Fulfilling Your God-Given Purpose

Harrison House
Shippensburg, PA

A *Sparkling Gems from the Greek*
Guided Devotional for Your Divine Destiny

Fulfilling Your God-Given *Purpose*

Rick Renner

 Scripture quotations are taken from the King James Version. All emphasis within Scripture quotations is the author's own.

Published by Harrison House Publishers
Shippensburg, PA 17257

ISBN 13 TP: 978-1-6675-1518-2

ISBN 13 eBook: 978-1-6675-1519-9

For Worldwide Distribution, Printed in the U.S.A.

1 2 3 4 5 6 7 8 / 30 29 28 27 26

Contents

Day 1

Whose Faith Are You Following?

That ye be not slothful, but followers of them who through faith and patience inherit the promises.

— Hebrews 6:12

Let me ask you a question today: Who is the most influential spiritual leader in your life right now? Is there one leader whom you respect and admire so exceptionally that you would want to emulate him and try to be like him in your own life? Is there one certain leader producing the type of fruit you long to see generated in your own personal life? If so, who is that leader?

You may wonder if it's right to follow someone so closely that you actually start emulating them. But the Bible is replete with scriptures that instruct us to be followers of spiritual leaders. One such scripture is Hebrew 6:12: "That ye be not slothful, but followers of them who through faith and patience inherit the promises."

Notice that this scripture says we are to be "*...follower*s of them who through faith and patience inherit the promises." The word "followers" is taken from the Greek word *mimetes,* from which we get the English word *imitate.* Other words that are derived from *mimetes* are "mimic" and "mime." However, the best translation of this word is actually the word "actor."

Therefore, the command to "follow" isn't referring to a casual type of following; rather, it implies an intentional study of the deeds, words, actions, and thoughts of another person in an attempt to fully understand that person and then to replicate his attributes in one's own life. This type of *following* enables a person to think like his subject, walk like his subject, mimic his subject's movements, make the vocal intonations of his subject, and act like his subject in a masterful way. However, this can only be achieved by those seriously committed to the act of *replication.* Such a commitment to act, mimic, or replicate a respected leader is the result of true discipleship.

Therefore, you could actually translate this phrase:

> *"...But skillfully and convincingly act like those who through faith and patience inherit the promises."*

A good actor studies the character and life of another and then portrays that person on a stage or on film. The actor obtains every bit of information he possibly can about the person in order to better portray him in his acting role. Then the actor begins to practice acting just like that person — trying to talk like him, think like him, and even walk and dress like him. If the actor acts long enough and consistently enough, the character role he is playing can actually become a part of the actor's own identity. That's the power of acting!

The writer of Hebrews understood the power of imitation. That's why he said in essence, "If you want to walk in faith, find someone who successfully walks in faith. Watch what he says, how he behaves, and how he lives — and then act like him! Do what he does; say what he says; and behave like he behaves. Be an imitator of those who through faith and patience have inherited the promises!"

You may ask, "But isn't it hypocritical to act like I feel great when I really feel bad?" Absolutely not! Acting and imitating are foundational to the Christian life. It is for this very reason you are instructed to "...put ye on the Lord Jesus Christ, and make not provision for the flesh..." (Romans 13:14). When you wake up in the morning, you may not feel like smiling, talking, or saying anything nice to anyone. But because you want to please the Lord, what do you do? You choose to be nice, to smile, to speak kindly; in other words, you choose to put on the Lord Jesus Christ. You make the decision to act differently than you naturally feel.

Putting on Christ is a daily mindset — a daily, hour-by-hour determination. So wake up and declare that you have the mind of Christ! Find some godly people who live according to who they truly are in the Spirit — new creations with the nature, character, desires, and behavior of Jesus Christ. Study their lives, and follow their example. In other words, ACT like those who through faith and patience inherit the promises!

My Prayer for Today

Lord, I need an example that I can follow and imitate! Your Word commands me to imitate strong and successful spiritual leaders, so I am asking You to help me find that exact leader whom You want me to follow and imitate. Give me the grace to do what he does, say what he says, and act the way he acts, until finally I no longer have to act because I have become like the person I have been imitating. Holy Spirit, I want to be obedient to God's Word. Since God tells me to mimic those who through faith and patience inherit the promises of God, I'm asking You to please help me recognize the people to whom I should look as spiritual examples in my walk with God. I pray this in Jesus' name!

My Confession for Today

I confess that I do not have to find my way by myself! By locating godly examples, I can imitate these people's lives and produce the same fruit they produce in their lives. So right now I choose to follow the examples of those who have preceded me —acting like them and replicating both their acts and their godly fruit in my life. God's Word says this is what I am to do, so I will do as I am commanded. The Holy Spirit will help me know exactly who should be the supreme examples in my life, and He will help me follow their example as I ought to do. I declare this by faith in Jesus' name!

Questions for You to Consider

1. Who is the most influential spiritual leader in your life right now? Have you ever taken the time to let that leader know that you appreciate him?

2. What have you done to establish a relationship with that leader? Write down ideas regarding what you can do to strengthen your relationship with him.

3. What in particular do you respect about this leader, and what fruit is demonstrated in his life that you want to see reproduced in your own life? Take the time to really think about this question, and write down your answers.

Day 2

Present Your Bodies a Living Sacrifice

> *I beseech you therefore, brethren, by the mercies of God, that ye present your bodies a living sacrifice, holy, acceptable unto God, which is your reasonable service.*
>
> — Romans 12:1

When Mary's days of purification were finished after the miraculous birth of Jesus, Luke 2:22 tells us that Mary and Joseph brought their Son to Jerusalem to dedicate Him to the Lord. It says, "And when the days of her purification according to the law of Moses were accomplished, they brought him to Jerusalem, to present him to the Lord."

Mary and Joseph came to Jerusalem with the express purpose "to present" the young Jesus to God. To make such a journey to Jerusalem required finances to pay for the journey itself and to purchase the turtledoves and pigeons that would be offered to God at the time they presented Jesus. This was no casual, accidental, haphazard, unplanned event. Presenting Jesus to the Lord in the temple was a serious occasion, as it was for all males in Israel. Such an event was planned in advance and done with great reverence toward God. Thus, it was a very hallowed, consecrated, holy moment as Joseph and Mary approached the temple at the time set for Jesus' dedication.

Luke 2:22 says that Joseph and Mary came "...to present him to the Lord." The word "present" comes from the Greek word *paristimi*, which is a compound of the words *para* and *istimi*. The prefix *para* means "alongside," and the word *istimi* means "to place." When these two words are compounded together, the new word means to place beside; to place at one's disposal; to surrender; to offer, as to offer a sacrifice to God; or to present, as to present a special offering to God. This word undoubtedly communicates the fact that Mary and Joseph were coming to the temple on this day to intentionally place their newborn son into God's close care. They were dedicating and entrusting Him into God's protection. They were surrendering Him to God's supervision and making a pledge that this new baby boy was God's possession and that God could therefore use Him however He wished.

This Greek word *paristimi* ("present") is precisely the same word that Paul used in Romans 12:1, when he wrote, "I beseech you therefore, brethren, by the mercies of God, that ye present your bodies a living sacrifice, holy, acceptable unto God, which is your reasonable service." The fact that Paul used this same word sheds some very important light on Romans 12:1.

First, we know that Paul was very earnest when he wrote Romans 12:1 because he began by solemnly telling them, "I beseech you...." The word "beseech" comes from the Greek word *parakaleo*. The word *parakaleo* is a Greek compound of the words *para* and *kaleo*. The word *para* means "alongside," and the word *kaleo* means "to call" or "to beckon." When these two words are compounded together, the new word pictures one who comes alongside someone else, as close as he can get, and then begins to passionately call out, plead, beckon, beg, and beseech that other person to do something on his behalf.

In many places, the word *parakaleo* is used to depict "a person who is earnestly praying." Therefore, the word *parakaleo* is also a word that can depict "a person who is sincerely expressing his heart to God in prayer." In light of this fact, one Greek scholar says that it is almost as if the apostle Paul dropped to his knees in this verse and began to prayerfully plead for his Roman readers to hear his petition. His heartfelt request was that they would present their bodies as a living sacrifice to God.

It must be noted that the word *parakaleo* also described what military commanders did before they sent their troops into battle. After summoning the troops together, their commander would beseech or exhort them as he warned them of the realities of warfare. The commander would describe in detail what they were going to face in their battle; then he'd urge them to keep on fighting bravely until the victory was won. All of this is included in the word *parakaleo*.

This is very significant in the context of Romans 12:1. Paul was urging believers to dedicate their bodies to God. However, Paul knew that when a believer makes the decision to dedicate his body to God, the carnal nature may respond by going to war against the spirit. The flesh just doesn't want to submit to the law of God or to do what God wishes. So when Paul besought his readers to yield their bodies to God, he was also warning them that such an action might stir up a battle in the flesh.

The carnal nature has long been the driving force for what is done with the body; therefore, it will most likely rebel when it is told to submit to God's control. This is why anyone who decides to present and dedicate his body to God must be ready and willing to fight the battle with the flesh until victory is achieved.

As mentioned earlier, Paul uses the Greek word *paristimi* when he says we are to "present" our bodies as a living sacrifice. This is exactly the same word used in Luke 2:22 to depict that moment when Jesus' parents presented baby Jesus to God in the temple at Jerusalem. Just as Jesus' dedication was no casual, accidental, haphazard, unplanned event, now Paul is telling us that the presentation of our bodies to God is a serious occurrence in our lives. This is no light affair, but one that should be done in a very hallowed, consecrated, and serious manner. It is a crucial, historical moment in our lives when we intentionally place ourselves in God's close care. We surrender ourselves and all that we are to God's supervision, making a solemn pledge that we are His and that He can therefore use us in whatever way He wishes.

You may wrongly assume that because you are a believer, this act of surrender has already occurred. But just because you are a believer does not mean that you have completely surrendered your body to God. If becoming a believer automatically caused this act of surrender to take place, Paul wouldn't have found it necessary to earnestly urge the Roman believers to do it.

Notice that we are to present ourselves as a "living sacrifice." In the Old Testament, an animal sacrifice would be offered upon the altar. Because the animal was dead, it could only be presented to the Lord once as a sacrificial offering.

But in the New Testament, we are urged to present ourselves to God as a *living* sacrifice. This implies that we must live in a continual state of surrender and consecration. Our commitment may begin with a momentous, "once-and-for-all" decision, but it must be followed with a daily decision to keep on surrendering ourselves to the Lord. Thus, we must see every day of our lives as another day — another opportunity — to yield our lives to God.

Each new day necessitates new surrender and consecration. What you surrendered to God yesterday is already old. Today is a new day and demands a new and higher level of consecration.

Therefore, as you awake each morning, train yourself to begin your day with a prayer of consecration in which you solemnly and in holy reverence present yourself and all that you are to God's purposes. Don't assume that because you did it yesterday, you don't need to do it today. What you did yesterday remains in yesterday's sphere. Each new day beckons you to take a step closer to the Lord and to make a commitment more serious than the one you made before.

Have you willfully, deliberately, and intentionally presented your body to God? Just as Jesus' parents brought Him to the Temple to present Him to the Lord, God is asking you to reverently come into His Presence to offer yourself as a living sacrifice to be used for His purposes. If you haven't ever taken this step of faith, are you ready to take it now? The carnal nature may declare war when you make the decision to surrender completely to the Lord, so be prepared to deal with the flesh. Just determine that you will not stop until the victory has been won!

Today is the day to surrender yourself into the hands of God. Don't wait until tomorrow — and don't depend on what you did yesterday. This is a new day, and God is calling you to surrender yourself anew. So don't let ANYTHING hold you back from taking this step of faith right now!

My Prayer for Today

Lord, today I am surrendering myself as a living sacrifice to be used in whatever way You choose. I know You are beckoning me to come higher and closer than ever before, so right now I approach You with great reverence and surrender myself more fully to You. With all my heart, I vow to give You my soul, my emotions, my spirit, my body, and everything else that I am and that I possess. I want to live for You and to serve You for the rest of my life. Starting today, I yield to You completely. When You speak, I will do exactly what You tell me to do. I pray this in Jesus' name!

My Confession for Today

I confess that I am surrendered to the purposes of God. I daily consecrate myself to God — to do what He wants and to live a life pleasing to Him. My flesh may try to wage war against this consecration, but I take authority over my flesh, and I tell it what to do. My body does not control me. Instead, I control it, using it as my instrument to do whatever God asks me to do. Every day when I awake, I renew my consecration and personal commitment to serve God with all my heart. I am His completely, and I will obey whatever His Spirit prompts me to do. I declare this by faith in Jesus' name!

Questions for You to Consider

1. Has there been a moment in your life when you seriously consecrated yourself more fully to God's purposes? When was that moment? How did this deeper commitment affect your life?

2. Do you daily consecrate yourself to the Lord? If the answer is no, how long has it been since you dropped to your knees and reverently surrendered your life, your mind, your emotions, your talents, your money, your family, your job, your friends, your plans, and all that you are to the Lord?

3. Would God say that you live your life like a "living sacrifice"?

Day 3

Run Like You Are in the Race of Your Life!

Know ye not that they which run in a race run all, but one receiveth the prize? So run, that ye may obtain.

—1 Corinthians 9:24

The main goal of all believers should be to find God's plan for their lives and then to go after it with all their might and strength. But most Christians have never even awakened to the fact that God has a special race for them to run! This is why Paul asked the Corinthians, "Know ye not that they which run in a race run all, but only one receiveth the prize? So run, that ye may obtain."

Paul teaches us here that we are in a "race." The word "race" is the Greek word *stadion*, which later became our word "stadium." However, it first described a race course that was 600 feet in length or one-eighth of a Roman mile — the exact length that was used in the Olympics of the ancient world and in the Isthmian Games that were held near the city of Corinth. Because Paul was highly educated, he knew precisely what he was doing when he used a word that described the Olympic race course of his day.

As noted above, eventually the word *stadion* became the word for a stadium, a place where athletic competitions were held. Since this is the picture Paul has in his mind as he uses the word "race," let's stop to consider the Olympic competitions and competitors of that time.

The winners of the Olympic competitions were rewarded both materially and with great honor; however, if you study the Olympic champions in the ancient world, you will see that the primary emphasis of reward was not on material wealth, but on the distinguished honor bestowed on the winners. These people were only able to achieve victory in the Olympic games by being disciplined, balanced, and committed to excellence; for these qualities, they were held in high regard. They became revered as heroes, gods, or icons in their society. Respect, honor, notoriety, and fame became their lifelong reward.

In addition to these ideas, it is also important to note that the word "race," from the Greek word *stadion*, depicted the huge arena where athletic competitions were held. Paul uses this word to tell us that when we enter the race of faith, it puts us in the center of the arena. People see us as we walk by faith. They know of our struggles, and they watch as spectators to see if we will win our battles.

We must always keep in mind, therefore, that we're not running a private race of faith, but a race that has influence on many people's lives. Hence, Paul urges us to run our race in a way that encourages the bystanders who are watching from the sidelines to jump into the race themselves and pursue their destiny in God!

By using these ideas, Paul was communicating to the Corinthians (and to us) that we need to see ourselves as spiritual Olympic competitors! This life we lead is no game; it is the most serious competition we will ever face in this world. The rewards of a life well lived are enormous. Not only will God materially reward us as we are faithful to His call, but He also reserves eternal rewards of honor and glory for those of us who run our race well in this life (Romans 2:10).

It is interesting that Paul says, "...They which run in a race run all...." Notice particularly the emphasis "run all." It means every believer is in some kind of race. A believer may not have awakened to the race he is in yet, or perhaps the race hasn't yet been revealed to him. Nevertheless, the fact remains that God has a specific plan for every individual.

Our task is to find the divine plan for our lives; to get in shape so we can start running our race; and then to run like mad so we can finish in first place! That's why Paul exhorted us, "...Run, that ye may obtain" (1 Corinthians 9:24).

You see, runners have one thought foremost in their minds — the finish line! With this analogy in mind, Paul tells you to run your spiritual race with all your might, keeping your focus on the goal — the divine call on your life as God has revealed it to you. You may ask, "How long am I supposed to keep running and trying to reach my God-given goals?" The answer is until you "obtain" what God called you to do!

The word "obtain" is the Greek word *katalambano*, which is a compound of two words, *kata* and *lambano*. The word *kata* describes "something that is coming downward," and the word *lambano* means "to take or to seize something." When compounded together into one word, *katalambano* means "to grab hold of, to seize, to wrestle, to pull down, and to finally make a desired object your very own." This is the picture of someone who finally sees what he wants — and instead of letting that goal he desires slip away, he pounces on it, seizing it and latching hold of it with all his might!

Paul uses this word *katalambano* to depict the attitude of a runner who is running with all his energy, straining forward as he keeps his focus fixed on the finish line. At last the runner reaches the goal, and the prize is now his! He gave that race all he had to give, and it paid off! Had he approached the race with a casual, lazy attitude, the prize would have gone to another. But because he ran to obtain that prize, in the end that's exactly what he did!

There is no doubt that you have a divine purpose for your life, something God has called you to do. God has marvelous ideas and plans for your life! The question is this: Do you want to fulfill His plans for you? If your answer is truly yes, then set your heart on your goal. Don't be half-hearted, mealymouthed, touchy, or easily discouraged. It's time for you to develop some resolve!

Do you see yourself as someone who is running the spiritual Olympic event of his or her life? Or are you simply "jogging for Jesus"? If you're serious about fulfilling God's plan for your life, it's time to shift into high gear and to start putting all your spiritual, mental, and physical energies into getting the job done. You have to remove all distractions and commit yourself to a life of discipline, balance, and devotion.

Your attitude must be, "I'm going to run this race, and I'm going to WIN it! I'm not going to live my whole life missing out on what God has for me! No matter what inconvenience I endure, what price I have to pay, or what adjustments I have to make, I am going to faithfully run my race so that one day I can obtain the prize — the fulfillment of God's call on my life!"

My Prayer for Today

Lord, I want to set my eyes on the finish line and never lose my focus until I know that I've accomplished the task You have given me to do. I know it's going to take all my spiritual, mental, and physical energies to get this job done. So I am turning to You now, Holy Spirit, and I'm asking You to empower me and to help me make it all the way to the completion of the dream You have given to me! I pray this in Jesus' name!

My Confession for Today

I declare that I have a divine purpose in life! I am not half-hearted, mealy-mouthed, touchy, or easily discouraged. I am like a runner who is seriously running a race. Because I'm serious about achieving God's plan for my life, I am shifting into high gear and putting all my spiritual, mental, and physical energies into getting the job done. I declare this by faith in Jesus' name!

Questions for You to Consider

1. Do you know what race you are supposed to be running in your life?

2. Are you running that race with 100 percent of your effort, or are you just half-heartedly jogging along in your life?

3. For you to achieve what God has told you to do, what changes of attitude and behavior do you need to make in your life? Write these changes down so you can pray about them!

Day 4

Become More Determined Than Hell Itself!

> *Are they ministers of Christ? (I speak as a fool) I am more; in labours more abundant, in stripes above measure, in prisons more frequent, in deaths oft.*
>
> —2 Corinthians 11:23

I am often amazed by people who say they want to be mightily used by God but yet are so "soft"! It doesn't take much at all to ruffle these people's feathers. A little inconvenience or discomfort is enough to upset them and start them complaining. And if they are asked to do a little extra work for free, they act like martyrs who are doing something extremely sacrificial!

If you're going to do something mighty for God, you have to throw yourself into the call of God and do what is needed, regardless of whether or not it is convenient to you. The fact is, doing what God has called us to do must be paramount in our lives — more important than any comfort or pleasure. Like the examples we see in the lives of Jesus and the apostle Paul, we must be willing to do anything required or go to any length to do exactly what God has assigned to us.

Of course, God wants His people to be blessed! But a believer shouldn't start whining and complaining just because he runs into an attack of the devil that affects the level of comfort he is accustomed to. And if he's asked to do a little more than what is usually asked of him, he shouldn't start griping that the extra task is not part of his job description. When a person does that, we can know that this is someone who will not do something mighty for God — at least not until he makes an adjustment in his attitude!

To push the forces of hell out of the way, you have to be more determined than hell itself. You have to be willing to do anything necessary to get the job done. The vision before you must be more important than your own personal pleasure. When you adopt this mentality for your life, you will always push through hard times and take significant territory for the Kingdom of God.

Paul then goes on to tell us more about his determined attitude to finish God's call, regardless of what he has to do to finish it, and the challenges he has to face on his way to victory.

Stripes Above Measure

In addition to working hard, Paul tells us what he has physically endured in order to fulfill his heavenly assignment. He tells us that he has been physically beaten as he pursued the fulfillment of his God-given task, experiencing "...stripes above measure...."

The word "stripes" is the Greek word *plege*. It means "to smite, to hit, to wound," or "to violently strike." There are many examples of this word in the New Testament. In Luke 10:30, Jesus tells us, "And Jesus answering said, A certain man went down from Jerusalem to Jericho, and fell among thieves, which stripped him of his raiment, and wounded him, and departed, leaving him half dead." The word "wounded" is this Greek word *plege*.

Notice that the man's wounds were so devastating that when the thieves departed, they assumed he was dead. These were mortal wounds. Now Paul uses this same word to describe the kinds of beatings he received as he sought to fulfill his God-given assignment in life.

This word is also used in Acts 16:33 to describe the kind of beating Paul and Silas received in Philippi. After God's power shook the prison walls and set Paul and Silas free, the keeper of the prison came to them to ask how to be saved. Acts 16:33 tells us that once the prison guard was saved, he "...took them the same hour of the night, and washed their *stripes*...." This word "stripes" is the same Greek word *plege*. Here we see an example of the physical beatings Paul endured.

But this incident in Philippi was just one example of Paul being physically knocked around by opponents to the Gospel. In Second Corinthians 11:23, he goes on to say that he experienced these stripes "above measure."

The words "above measure" are from the Greek word *huperballo*. It is a compound of the words *huper* and *ballo.* The word *huper* means "above and beyond what is normal." The word *ballo* means "to throw." And when these two words are joined together, they depict "a very powerful picture"!

Imagine an archer who takes his bow and arrows to the field for target practice. He aims his arrow at the bull's-eye, pulls back on his bow, and shoots the arrow. But he misses his target and shoots way over the top or exceedingly out of range. The arrow flies way beyond the range of anything considered normal. This pictures the meaning of the Greek word *huperballo*.

Paul's use of this word tells us that he was beaten way beyond the range of what we could even begin to imagine. The word *huperballo* describes both the frequency and the intensity of his beatings. The beatings Paul received occurred frequently. They were cruel, severe, merciless acts of brutality. What Paul's enemies did to his body was way over the top! But Paul never allowed even these acts of physical brutality to affect his commitment to the task God had given him.

You must be more determined than the forces that will try to come against you. Otherwise, it won't take much pressure to make you say, "This is too hard" or "I didn't understand how difficult this was going to be." You'll mentally start packing your bags so you can transfer back to more comfortable territory where less is expected of you.

By no means am I wishing hardships or hard times on you. But I do pray that you make up your mind to be tougher than anything the devil ever tries to throw in your direction. In your flesh alone, you are not strong enough to withstand the devil's assaults. But with the power of the Holy Spirit, you can resist, stand against, and drive back everything the devil will attempt to do to you, to your family, to your business, or to your church or ministry. Isn't it time for you to make up your mind to stick with God's call on your life and press ahead in the power of the Holy Spirit?

Prisons More Frequent

Paul goes on to tell us that he has been "...in prisons more frequent...." The word "prison" is the Greek word *plulake*. It describes "a place of custody, a prison ward," or "a place heavily guarded by keepers and watchmen." Such a prison was usually a small, dark chamber in which the most hardened, dangerous, and menacing prisoners were confined. The prisoners who were put into this particular kind of chamber were considered so risky that they were usually accompanied by a host of prison guards who guarded them 24 hours a day.

This word *plulake* ("prison") is used in Acts 12:4 for Peter's imprisonment in Jerusalem. Acts 12:4 tells us, "And when he had apprehended him, he put him in prison, and delivered him to four quaternions of soldiers to keep him; intending after Easter to bring him forth to the people." Peter must have been viewed as especially risky to have four quaternions of soldiers assigned to keep watch over him!

Paul was also kept in this kind of extreme confinement many times during his ministry; this is what he means when he says here that he has been in "prisons more frequent." In fact, Paul became so familiar with this type of confinement that he even spent his final days under similar circumstances: "And when we came to Rome, the centurion delivered the prisoners to the captain of the guard: but Paul was suffered to dwell by himself with a soldier that kept him" (Acts 28:16).

No one wants to go to jail! But if going to jail meant that Paul would accomplish his apostolic calling along the way, that was what he was willing to do. Paul was ready to undergo any inconvenience, pay any price, and go to all lengths to do what God had commissioned him to do. Even jail would not stop him.

Deaths Oft

In addition to the beatings and imprisonments he endured, Paul also says he was "...in deaths oft." The word "deaths" is from the Greek word *thanatos*. Here, however, Paul uses the plural form, *thanatoi*, which is literally translated "deaths."

We know that Paul wrote in First Corinthians 15:31, "…I die daily." We tend to spiritualize this statement, but in reality, Paul faced actual physical death on a regular basis. When he wrote, "…I die daily," he actually meant, "I am constantly confronted with the prospect of death."

Paul faced death so often that he learned how to face it bravely. In Romans 14:8, he wrote, "…whether we die, we die unto the Lord…." In First Corinthians 15:55, we see that he learned to meditate on victory rather than on mortality and fatality: "O death, where is thy sting? O grave, where is thy victory?" These are not allegorical verses about death. They are the thoughts of a man who faced the prospect of death almost on a daily basis.

Paul never sought to live under this constant threat of murder or execution. It was just a part of the journey to get where he needed to go. But rather than run and hide from imminent danger, he faced it bravely and kept moving forward to do what he was called to do.

Had Paul been less committed, it would have taken only a few of these difficult experiences to knock him out of the race. But because he was totally focused on finishing the assignment Heaven had given him, he pushed beyond each of these attacks, and at the end of his life, he was able to say, "…I have finished my course…" (2 Timothy 4:7).

The Holy Spirit who empowered the apostle Paul to overcome each of these instances is the same Holy Spirit who is available to help you. You never have to be a defeated victim. If you choose to take advantage of the power that is available to you, the Spirit of God will energize and lift you to a place of victory over any obstacle the devil tries to throw in your way. Never forget that you have resurrection power residing inside you (*see* Romans 8:11). If you yield to that power, it will supernaturally quicken you to overcome every time!

So throw open your arms of faith and embrace the Spirit's power to overcome each attack the devil has tried to orchestrate against you. If you embrace that power, it will begin to flood you with everything you need to survive and to gloriously succeed in your task! Make the decision to let it start flowing today!

My Prayer for Today

Lord, I thank You that because Your Spirit lives in me, I have everything I need to overcome any attack the devil would try to orchestrate against me. Because Your resurrection power resides in me, I am stronger than the devil; I am tougher than any problem; and I can outlast any time of difficulty. It is not a question of IF I will win, but of WHEN I will win the victory! I thank You for giving me the power of the Holy Spirit to outlast every attack and to persist until I have accomplished what You have asked me to do! I pray this in Jesus' name!

My Confession for Today

I confess that I am totally focused on finishing the assignment Heaven has given to me. I will successfully push beyond each attack of the enemy because the Holy Spirit is empowering me. I don't have to be a defeated victim. I choose to take advantage of the power that is available to me. Therefore, the Spirit of God will energize and lift me to a place of victory over any obstacle the devil tries to throw in my way. I have resurrection power residing inside me, and it supernaturally quickens me to overcome every demonic attack that tries to assault me and my purpose in life! I declare this by faith in Jesus' name!

Questions for You to Consider

1. Was there a time in your past when you felt extremely weak, but then the Spirit of God suddenly quickened you with such divine energy that you became supernaturally strong to overcome a difficult challenge in your life? If yes, what was that occasion when divine power flooded you so strongly?

____

____

____

____

____

____

2. Can you verbalize the changes that occurred in you when God's power infused you with new strength? Were there immediate changes in your attitudes? Did it have an impact on your ability to endure?

____

____

____

____

____

____

3. How was that difficult situation resolved as a result of the supernatural empowerment you experienced?

Day 5

God Isn't Looking for Aristocrats, Cultured, or High-Born People

For ye see your calling, brethren, how that not many wise men after the flesh, not many mighty, not many noble, are called: But God hath chosen the foolish things of the world to confound the wise....

—1 Corinthians 1:26-27

Through the ages, God has always delighted in choosing normal people to do His business. If you consider yourself to be a normal, average kind of person, that means you are just the kind of person God is looking to use!

First Corinthians 1:26 says, "For ye see your calling, brethren, how that not many wise men after the flesh, not many mighty, not many noble...." Do you see the word "noble" in this verse? It comes from the Greek compound word *eugenes*. The first part of the word is the Greek prefix *eu*, which means "well" or "good." The second part of the word is the Greek word *genes*, from which we get our English word for the human gene. When these two words are compounded together, the new word portrays people who are well-born or who have excellent genes.

In ancient Greece, the word *eugenes* meant men of high descent, such as sons of kings, politicians, or others from the upper crust of society. It referred to individuals whose ancestors had been powerful, wealthy, rich, or famous. These were high-born, blue-blooded, cultured, refined, courtly, pedigreed, aristocratic people who sustained their lofty positions in society based on their birth.

Examples of this class of people would be members of royalty who held their exalted positions in society whether or not they personally merited those positions. They were born into the upper crust and stayed there simply because of their family name or relations.

Modern examples of *eugenes* are sons and daughters of kings and queens who retain their royal posts simply because of the blood that runs in their veins. Other examples would be the sons and daughters of famous and beloved politicians. Although the offspring themselves may not have accomplished anything significant, their famous last name has sealed their fame and place in society. They were born with a "name" that gives them lifetime guarantees and access to privileges that are not available to common people with unknown names.

But the word *eugenes* can also refer to people who carry the seed of genius as a result of the good genes with which they were born. An example of this category of *eugenes* would be the family of Albert Einstein.

Some years ago, I was visiting a pastor in New York City who told me an interesting story about a visit he had with the niece of Albert Einstein. He was amazed to discover she had five earned doctorates and held several prominent positions in universities in New York City. Like her uncle, Albert, she was endowed with genius in her genes, and it carried her all the way to the top of every field in which she became involved.

Let me give you another example of "good genes" as portrayed by the Greek word *eugenes*. Before the Russian revolution, noble families owned the lands and controlled the territory of Russia. In 1917 when the Red Army seized power, all of Russia's rich decoration and regal royalty came to an abrupt end. The nobility was killed or fled to foreign countries. It looked as if history had buried them forever.

Thank God, today the communist regime is gone. In its place, a brand-new rich Russian class is emerging. People often ask, "Who are these new super-rich Russians?" It is interesting to note that many of them have the same family names of the old ruling class that dominated Russia before the 1917 revolution. The nobility that runs in their veins is too strong to be held down. Once again, it is taking them to the top of society.

The Russian nobility were endowed with powerful genes. These genes have been passed down to the present generation. Now the offspring of the Russian nobles are reassuming positions of power that were once occupied by their grandparents. This tendency to rule and reign is in their genes.

The word *eugenes* describes both kinds of people — those born into famous families who enjoy the inherent privileges of their last name, and those who carry a streak of genius, talent, or superiority in their genes. These are "the upper crust" — the ruling class or aristocracy of the world.

However, Paul says that God hasn't specialized in calling this category of people. Take a look at world history, and you'll see that God hasn't primarily specialized in using kings, queens, royalty, politicians, scientists, philosophers, writers, movie stars, or celebrities to advance His Kingdom. From the onset of time, God has reached into the hearts of ordinary men and women. These are the ones who most often accomplish mighty feats through His grace and power.

So if God isn't looking for the upper crust of society, He must be looking to "the lower crust" in other words, to the ordinary, usual, regular, routine, run-of-the-mill, standard, typical kind of people. This means that if you come from a normal, average background, you are possibly the very one God wants to use!

Yes, God has called the rich and famous as well, but it is the regular folks who most often find themselves chosen by God to carry out His will on earth. He specializes in using ordinary people, just like you and me. That is why Paul goes on to say, "But God hath chosen the foolish things of the world to confound the wise...."

The word "foolish" is from the Greek word *moraino*. The word "moron" also comes from this Greek word. My thesaurus gives these other synonyms for a "moron": idiot, imbecile, halfwit, numskull, dimwit, dunce, blockhead, dope, ignoramus, lamebrain, jerk, or twerp!

The truth is, no one is an idiot in God's view. But the world often views people whom God chooses as being nitwits, lamebrains, and idiots. It is worth noting that the word *moraino* was used in Paul's time to "depict people whom the world scorned, made fun of, and treated with contempt."

Because much of the Early Church was comprised of servants and slaves, most of the people in the local congregations were very uneducated, uncultured, clumsy, crude, awkward, and unpolished. It wasn't that they were stupid. They had simply never been exposed to or taught about manners, culture, and refined behavior. Reared and treated as servants since birth, they'd never had a need to know these skills.

However, the early Christians' lack of polish made them look stupid in the world's eyes. In fact, the Roman Empire at first looked upon Christianity as the religion of stupid, poor people because it grew so rapidly among the lower slave classes.

Yet Paul says, "...God hath chosen the foolish things of the world to confound the wise...." The word "confound" is the Greek word *kataishuno*. It means "to put to shame, to embarrass, to confuse, to frustrate, or to baffle." The word "wise" is again the word *sophos*, referring to those who are "naturally brilliant, intellectually sharp," or "especially enlightened." Paul is saying that God calls people whom the world considers morons in order to put to shame, embarrass, confuse, frustrate, and baffle those who think they're so smart!

So if anyone has ever called you an idiot — if you've ever been called a stupid imbecile, a jerk, or a twerp — it's time for you to rejoice! *This makes you a candidate to be used for God's glory!*

The following expanded version of First Corinthians 1:26-27 gives a fuller picture of the Greek words used in this verse:

> *For you see your calling, brothers, how not many of you were especially bright, educated, or enlightened according to the world's standards; not many of you were impressive; not many came from high-ranking families or from the upper crust of society. Instead, God selected people who are idiots in the world's view; in fact, the world sees them as imbeciles, jerks, real twerps. Yet God is using them to utterly confound those who seem smart in the world's eyes....*

Therefore, even though you may not have any genius residing in your genes nor any nobility running in your blood, that isn't a strike against you! You can't lay claim to these factors as excuses for not being used by God! God isn't looking for people who are geniuses or well-born, high-class blue bloods. He's looking for anyone who will say yes to His call! So if you consider yourself to be just a regular ol' person, it's time for you to start rejoicing again! You are exactly the kind of person God wants to use!

My Prayer for Today

Lord, help me stop making excuses for why I think God shouldn't use me! It's time for me to stop ignoring the call of God and to accept the fact that He has laid His hand upon me and wants to use me in this world. Forgive me for putting this off for so long, but today I accept Your call. I reject all excuses for any further delay, and I gladly embrace what You are telling me to do! I pray this in Jesus' name!

My Confession for Today

I boldly confess that I am exactly the kind of person Jesus Christ wants to use! I may not have the blue blood of nobility flowing through my veins, but I have been touched, cleansed, and redeemed by the blood of Jesus Christ. That blood qualifies me! With the Word as my guide and the Holy Spirit as my Teacher, I have everything I need to do anything Jesus ever requires of me. I am quick to obey; I do not hesitate; and I am faithful to carry out every assignment that He gives me! I boldly declare this in Jesus' name!

Questions for You to Consider

1. Thinking back on those who were most mightily used by God throughout the ages, do you know from which class of society most of them came?

2. Now think about those whom God is greatly using to touch the world and confound society today. What class of society do most of these people come from? What kind of education did most of them have when God first started using them in a notable way? How many of them have blue blood running in their veins or would be deemed geniuses by the great universities of the world?

3. What does this tell you about God's ability to use you?

Day 6

Where Does the Bible Ever Say God Is Looking for Brains?

For ye see your calling, brethren, how that not many wise men after the flesh, not many mighty, not many noble, are called: But God hath chosen the foolish things of the world to confound the wise; and God hath chosen the weak things of the world to confound the things which are mighty; And base things of the world, and things which are despised, hath God chosen....

—1 Corinthians 1:26-28

If you see yourself as weak, feeble, or unskilled, don't let that bother you too much. God has been calling feeble and unskilled people from the beginning of time. Few of those whom God has called have been the "cream of the crop" according to the flesh. Again and again, God has chosen people who were ill-esteemed in the eyes of the world when He needed a candidate or a group of people to do a job.

God has always used common people to build His Kingdom. He doesn't primarily choose famous movie stars or the royalty and nobility of the world to fulfill His plans and purposes on this earth. God's criteria are different from the criteria of the world. As Isaiah 55:8 says, "For my thoughts are not your thoughts, neither are your ways my ways, saith the Lord."

When God chose Samuel to lead the nation, Samuel was just a young boy. When God looked for someone to kill a giant, He chose a young shepherd boy named David. When the fullness of time came, and it was time to send His Son to earth, God chose a young girl named Mary to give birth to the Savior of the world.

When it was time for Jesus to choose disciples, He didn't go to the theological institutes or seminaries of the day. Rather, Jesus chose disciples who knew more about fishing and tax-collecting than about the Scriptures. And when God searched for someone He could use to write the majority of the New Testament, He chose the apostle Paul, who was once one of the meanest Christian killers of all time!

God has always shown up in places where He wasn't expected. Just consider the location where Jesus was born — in a lowly shepherd's stall. This was certainly not the place anyone would have expected the King of kings to be born. Wouldn't it have been better for the King of kings to be born in a gold-gilded hall with trumpets blasting to announce His birth?

So if you have ever thought you weren't good enough for God to use, it's time for you to renew your thinking! God is looking for people no one else wants or deems valuable. When great victories are won through ordinary folks, there's no question as to who should receive the glory! As First Corinthians 1:29 says, "That no flesh should glory in his presence."

The Old and New Testaments are filled with illustrations of people whom God wanted, but whom the world rejected. God's choice is not based on beauty or ugliness, talent or lack of talent, education or lack of education, a diploma or lack of a diploma. If a person has a right heart toward God, he is qualified to be used by God.

In First Corinthians 1:26-28, Paul wrote, "For ye see your calling, brethren, how that not many wise men after the flesh, not many mighty, not many noble, are called: but God hath chosen the foolish things of the world to confound the wise; and God hath chosen the weak things of the world to confound the things which are mighty; and base things of the world, and things which are despised, hath God chosen...."

As Paul writes his list of those whom God does and doesn't call, he begins by stating that God doesn't call many who are considered "wise" by the world. The word "wise" is from the Greek word *sophos*. It refers to a person who possesses "special enlightenment" or "special insight."

The word *sophos* was usually used to portray highly educated people, such as scientists, philosophers, doctors, teachers, and others who were considered to be the super-intelligentsia of the world. These belong to a class of individuals whom the world would call clever, astute, smart, or intellectually brilliant. This term was reserved only for those considered to be super-impressive or a cut above the rest of society.

But Paul says, "For ye see your calling, brethren, how that not many wise men after the flesh...." Paul informs us that most of the folks God calls don't fit into this category of the super-intelligentsia. In other words, God doesn't specialize in calling people who are especially bright, educated, astute, smart, or eminently enlightened.

I would be foolish to overlook the fact that over the years, many intelligent men and women who loved God have made a great impact on the world. Paul himself was a part of this elite group before he came to Christ. Apollos, Paul's friend who later pastored the church of Corinth, also came from this intellectual "upper echelon" of society. But Paul and Apollos were not typical of the First Century Church.

It was the *sophos* who scorned and ridiculed Paul when he preached in Athens. The philosophers of Athens, the Epicureans and the Stoics derided him and made him a laughingstock. Paul said that "not many" are called who fit into this *sophos* category. Of course, God's call is to all men; nevertheless, "not many" from this category respond to God's call.

Take a close look at the Early Church, and you'll see that it was primarily composed of servants, slaves, and poorer people who heard the Good News of the Gospel and believed. It was an army of common people. Although there were a few elite in the Church, these were the exception rather than the rule. In fact, as you study Church history, you will see that God specializes in calling people from a much lower class. And if you take a close look at the Church today, you'll see that God still specializes in calling common people.

Now, I'm not debasing education. People should get as much education as possible. But school-issued pieces of paper are not the criteria that impresses God and gets His attention. There have been many educated people whom God could not use. Even though they were brilliant according to the flesh, they were not worthy of being chosen because their hearts weren't right.

Educational degrees may help you get a good job and positively sway the opinion of men in your favor, but Paul makes it very clear that God is not bent on using people who are especially bright according to the standards of the flesh.

In fact, the Bible shows that when God does call people who are intellectually impressive, such as Moses or the apostle Paul, He usually has to empty them of themselves before He can use them! When they lean on their own understanding, they are unable to accomplish what God wants. But when they lean wholly upon Him, He is able to perform miracles through their lives.

Proverbs 3:5 says, "Trust in the Lord with all thine heart; and lean not unto thine own understanding." Certainly natural knowledge and understanding are needful in the world we live in today.

But if our natural understanding rather than our trust in God becomes the basis for our confidence, we put ourselves at a disadvantage. *We have to learn to use what we know while leaning only on the Lord and His might.*

David wrote, "Some trust in chariots, and some in horses: but we will remember the name of the Lord our God" (Psalm 20:7). The best technology of David's time was used to develop chariots. Man's greatest intellectual powers were employed to make chariots faster, stronger, and safer. In addition, horses represented natural power, strength, and might. Therefore, David was saying, "Some trust in man's mind and his great achievements; others rely on their own natural power and might; but we will rely upon the name of the Lord."

Perhaps you're one of those people who says, "God can't use me because I don't have enough gifts or talents. I haven't even been to college. I don't even have a Bible school degree." If you are, it's time for you to change the way you're thinking and talking. It's time for you to start seeing yourself the way God does!

In fact, if you feel inferior to others, remember that God regularly calls unskilled and uneducated people. Just think of the majority of the apostles whom Jesus hand-picked to serve at His side and to lay the foundation of the

Church. Those apostles were fishermen, tax collectors, common people — not theologians.

God is looking to build a strong, powerful army. The soldiers of an army are rarely composed of the intellectually astute. Flavius Vegetius Renatus, who lived around 380 AD, was the author of the most influential military book ever written for the Roman Empire. Look at the type of person he says makes the best soldier: "Peasants are the most fit to carry arms.... They are simple, content with little, inured to fatigue, and prepared in some measure for military life by their continual employment in farm work, in handling the spade, digging trenches, and carrying burdens."

The truth is, God is looking for people who know how and are willing to pay a price — to undergo any hardship needed, to confront the power of hell, and to "dig trenches and carry burdens" until their assignment is completed just as God ordered it. God doesn't necessarily need the super-intelligentsia of the world to get these jobs done. In fact, common people are often God's first choice because they are already equipped to a certain degree to face the challenges and difficulties of life.

So if you want to be used by God and serve in His army, quit complaining that you're not as smart or sharp as someone else. Where does the Bible ever say God is looking for brains? He's looking for hearts that are willing to follow Him. If you have that kind of heart, you are exactly the kind of person God wants to use!

My Prayer for Today

Lord, I am so glad You don't choose only the intellectually brilliant. You are looking for anyone who has a heart to be used by You. Well, that's me, Lord. I want You to use me. I offer You everything I have — my good points, my weak points, my gifts, my talents, and everything else that I am. I want You to use me for Your glory! I've told You before, but today I'm telling You again that I want You to take my life and do something wonderful with me! I pray this in Jesus' name!

My Confession for Today

I confess that I am exactly the kind of person God can use! God is looking to carry out great victories through my life! His choice is not based on beauty or a lack of beauty, talent or lack of talent, education or lack of education, a diploma or lack of a diploma. No, God has chosen me because I have a heart that is right before Him! I declare this in Jesus' name!

Questions for You to Consider

1. Can you recall concrete examples of people in the Bible whom the world thought to be worth nothing — yet God called them, changed them, and then used them to change world history? Try to name five people who fit into this category.

2. Can you think of specific people outside the Bible whom the world thought to be worth nothing, yet God used them to change society? Try to name five people who fit into this category as well.

3. If God specializes in calling people who come from common backgrounds, what does this mean for you?

Day 7

Coming into Compliance With God's Will

> *And he took with him Peter and the two sons of Zebedee, and began to be sorrowful and very heavy. Then saith he unto them, My soul is exceeding sorrowful, even unto death: tarry ye here, and watch with me. And he went a little farther, and fell on his face, and prayed, saying, O my Father, if it be possible, let this cup pass from me: nevertheless not as I will, but as thou wilt.*
>
> — Matthew 26:37-39

When God asks you to strike out into uncharted territory and accomplish something new and difficult, it can be challenging to bring your will into compliance with what He is asking you to do. Your mind will try to argue as if it knows best, and your flesh will try to drag its feet every step of the way. In these moments, you are faced with a defining moment in your life when you must place your trust in God's plan for your life and obey Him unconditionally.

I know this struggle intimately from experiences in my own life. When God first asked our family to move to the USSR, I knew He had something truly wonderful in store for us, but my flesh didn't relish the idea. Each night as I lay in bed, my mind would bombard me with a stream of negative thoughts of doubt and unbelief. My flesh would tell me, *Rick, this is the stupidest thing you could ever do in your life. If you really go through with this absurd notion, you will lose everything you have and never recover.* I remember asking God, "Are You really asking me to do this?"

At the time God called our family to the Soviet Union, our ministry in the United States was growing by leaps and bounds, and we were finally experiencing stability and success after many years of sacrifice. However, as good as our lives seemed at the time, God had something far bigger and more wonderful planned for our ministry, so He asked us to lay down our dream and trust in Him. As we entered this new, unfamiliar phase, we didn't understand His full design, but we chose to defer to His voice and trust that He knew what He was doing with our lives. And because we placed our trust in His divine plan and obeyed His call to move, our ministry exploded in ways that we could never have dreamed!

If you haven't yet run into one of these moments in your life, there will come a time in your future when you will have to step out and do what God is saying, even though you don't relish the idea of what He is asking you to do. In that moment, it is vital that you follow the guidance of the Holy Spirit so He can lead you into new realms of wonder and possibility.

In fact, the Bible tells us that Jesus Himself faced one of those moments in the Garden of Gethsemane. Matthew 26:37 and 38 relates, "And he took with him Peter and the two sons of Zebedee, and began to be sorrowful and very heavy. Then saith he unto them, My soul is exceedingly sorrowful, even unto death: tarry ye here, and watch with me." This passage of scripture reveals what took place as Jesus faced the horror of the Cross and all that He would have to endure in the atonement of mankind's sin. The reality of what the Father was asking Him to do was being brought to bear on Jesus, and it says He "...began to be sorrowful and very heavy" (v. 37). This word "sorrowful" is derived from the Greek word *lupeo,* which denotes "physical pain" or "emotional suffering." It can also be translated as broken-hearted, in despair, displeasure, downcast, grief, mournful, in pain, sorrowful, or wounded. It describes the intense grief of someone who has been wounded emotionally by a person or a situation.

Furthermore, the phrase "very heavy" in Matthew 26:37 is a translation of the Greek word *ademoneo,* which depicts "anguish, depression," or "dejection." The word "sorrowful" and the phrase "very heavy" are each sufficient on their own to convey the deep emotions Jesus was feeling in this moment of anguish. However, because they are used together, it is unmistakably clear that Jesus was tempted to be overwhelmed by the unimaginably hellish ordeal He was about to face. Although He had always known that the Cross was an integral part of His destiny on earth, it appears that the reality of His assignment weighed heavily upon His mind and body, and He was tempted to sway under the weight of it all.

In the following verse, Matthew wrote, "Then saith he unto them, My soul is exceedingly sorrowful, even unto death: tarry ye here, and watch with me" (Matthew 26:38). The word "soul" is the Greek word *psyche,* which denotes "the inner life, mental makeup, or emotions of an individual." The phrase "exceedingly sorrowful" is a translation of the Greek word *perilupeo,* which is a compound of the words *peri* and *lupeo.* The word *peri* means "around" or "to be surrounded," and *lupeo* is the same word we saw that describes "intense grief." When they are compounded in the context of this verse to form the word *perilupeo,* it tells us that Jesus was feeling nearly emotionally suffocated with despair as He faced the painful reality of God's plan for Him.

Then Matthew 26:39 continues, "And he went a little further, and fell on his face...." The stress and pressure Jesus was under was so heavy that He was able to go only "a little further" before He collapsed and "fell on his face." The force of the Greek language here indicates that Jesus literally collapsed under the weight of what He was experiencing. And as He fell, He fervently prayed, "...O my Father, if it be possible, let this cup pass from me: nevertheless not as I will, but as thou wilt" (v. 39).

However, in this intense moment as Jesus' soul was bombarded with mental and emotional anguish, He did not succumb to the will of His flesh. Rather, Jesus pushed through to embrace the will of God that He knew was His divine destiny. He surrendered and complied with the path the Father had set before Him, saying, "...Nevertheless, not as I will, but as thou wilt." Jesus was resolved to the Father's will rather than seek a way out of the situation.

The Father's plan for Jesus included His trials before the Sanhedrin, Herod Antipas, and Pontius Pilate, as well as Jesus being mocked, spit upon, scourged, and crucified. Although Jesus knew that the Father was faithful to Him and a glorious resurrection shortly awaited Him, this was the defining moment in His earthly life when trust and obedience were required in a measure greater than ever before. He had to "commit Himself" to God and trust that His heavenly Father would raise Him from the dead and deliver Him from the unspeakable horrors of spiritual darkness. Jesus could have rejected God's plan at this point, but He chose instead to bring His mind into compliance with the will of God. As a result of His obedience, He brought salvation to mankind through His sacrifice, and He was raised from the dead to sit at the Father's right hand as the Head of the Church and our eternal High Priest.

If Jesus Himself agonized over doing the will of the Father, then it should come as no surprise that we will wrestle with God's plan for our lives from time to time. Like Jesus, we must choose to push aside our reservations and commit to doing whatever God asks of us. We must learn to trust and obey.

If you follow your heavenly Father's plan, you will overcome any obstacle that tries to trip you up, and you will find yourself seated in a place of victory that you will never regret. It may be uncomfortable right now, but those emotions and struggles are temporary. They will pass, and when it's all said and done, you will be glad that you came into compliance with the will of God!

As I look back at the moment when God asked me to move my family to the USSR, I have no regrets. It was hard for my soul at the moment, but the victories won over many years make it clear that God only had good plans in store for us, even though it was difficult to understand that when it all began. Likewise, God has a good plan in store for you. He simply needs your compliance, trust, and obedience.

My Prayer for Today

Father, I ask You to help me push beyond my inward struggles concerning what You are asking me to do. Your requests have exposed my need to come up higher in my level of trust. This has revealed an area where I need to grow spiritually. Learning where I need to improve is good for me, so I thank You for leading me to this place where You can show me where I need to change and grow. Just as Jesus surrendered to Your will, I place my trust in You, and I will comply with Your plan regardless of how difficult it may be for me to understand in the moment. With the help of Your Spirit, I will trust and obey. I pray this prayer in Jesus' name!

My Confession for Today

I confess that God is faithful. If He is asking me to do something I don't completely understand, I can trust Him to have my best interest at heart. I don't need to be fearful of what He is telling me to do. I refuse to let my emotions get the best of me, and I choose to follow God's will for my life. I declare that I will not shrink back from the assignment God has given me, and I am determined that I will comply with His plan for my life! I declare this by faith in Jesus' name!

Questions for You to Consider

1. Can you think of an area of your life where God is asking you to comply with His plan and you're having a tough time obeying? What is that area, and what is specifically making it difficult for you to comply?

2. Do you know someone today who is struggling to do the will of God? What can you do to encourage that person? What personal experience of obeying God can you share to provoke that person to follow God's plan for his or her life?

3. What stands out in your mind regarding what you just read in this *Sparkling Gem?* What did you learn about Jesus and His time in the Garden of Gethsemane that you've never considered before?

Day 8

Do You Know What You Are Called to Do?

> *Not as though I had already attained, either were already perfect....*
>
> —Philippians 3:12

I have no doubt as to what God has called me to do with my life. He has called me to preach the Gospel and to help establish the Church in regions of the world that are unstable, difficult, and unchurched. That is my calling, and I am very confident of this fact. But for me to fulfill this divine call on my life requires hard work, attention, and a determination to never stop until I have achieved exactly what Jesus intended for me to achieve with my life.

When you look at the life of the apostle Paul, you'll find it very evident that he emphatically knew his calling. Furthermore, he was able to concretely express it and often wrote of it in his epistles. Over and over again, he wrote that he was an apostle to the Gentiles (Galatians 2:8). Paul lived, breathed, ate, slept, and awoke every day to the call of God that was on his life.

When Paul was in a Roman prison with the prospect of death staring him in the face, he never gave up because he knew he hadn't yet fulfilled the entire plan God had revealed to him. I personally believe that reaching his God-given goal was in Paul's mind when he wrote, "Not as though I had already attained, either were already perfect..." (Philippians 3:12).

The word "perfect" is the Greek word *teleo*. It refers to something that is "ripe, mature, perfect," or "complete." It suggests that Paul meant, "I have done a lot and accomplished much in comparison to others, but I haven't yet brought my assignment to completion. The job is not finished. I have not yet completed what God has called me to do."

During his multiple years of serving the Lord, Paul had achieved more than any other Christian leader of his time. He had preached on different continents, traveled to the countries of the Mediterranean Sea, and preached to governors and kings. Besides all these notable accomplishments, Paul had written the majority of the New Testament text! But none of this mattered to him because he knew he hadn't yet "attained" that for which Jesus Christ had apprehended him.

Instead of relaxing and taking it easy at the end of his life, Paul therefore turned his attention to the dream — to the unfulfilled vision or assignment that was still before him. Because there was still so much left to do, he went on to say, "...I follow after...." This phrase comes from the Greek word *dioko*, which is the word that is usually translated "to persecute." Let's stop and talk about this for a moment so we can understand the full force of what Paul was writing in this verse.

The word *dioko*, translated as "I follow after," is a fiercely aggressive word. In historic Greek literature, it means *to hunt; to pursue; to chase; to track down and kill.* It is the picture of an outdoorsman who is so determined to hunt down an animal that he will stop at nothing to pursue, chase, track down, and ultimately get his game!

Do hunters accidentally bag their game, or do they strategize in their plans to get a good one each hunting season? Hunters strategize! They dream! They talk to other hunters about the best places to hunt! They dress in camouflaged clothes; then they perch themselves high up on tree branches and wait for hours upon hours for an unlucky deer to walk into their trap. Once the deer comes in range, they shoot to kill! They hunt, hound, and stalk that animal until they finally kill it. Then they throw the big catch in the back of their truck and head home with their trophy—and the prospect of many good venison meals in their future! That is exactly what Paul means when he says, "I follow after."

The apostle Paul strategized, planned, studied, and ardently followed after the call of God on his life. You could say that he hunted, hounded, and stalked the call of God with all his heart, never stopping until he could say, "I got my game!" When Paul's job was finished, he gladly said, "...I have finished my course..." (2 Timothy 4:7). That's when he packed it all up and went home to Heaven with his trophy — a crown of reward.

For you to achieve what God has planned for your life, it will likewise require a fierce determination to keep pressing ahead. You can never stop until every part of your God-given assignment has been fulfilled. Jogging along at a comfortable pace will never get you where you need to go. You must focus your attention on the goal and then strategize, plan, and work until you can confidently say, "I've done exactly what Jesus wanted me to do!" But be forewarned: Achieving this goal will demand your utmost concentration and undivided attention and the empowerment of the Holy Spirit. Do you know God's plan for your life?

Do you know the assignment He has designed just for you? Are you following after that divine call with all your heart? If not, today is the perfect time to start discovering and then following after God's call on your life!

My Prayer for Today

Lord, I am asking You to help me really know my calling so I can ardently follow after it with all my might. Help me push all distractions out of my way and to put my sights on fulfilling the assignment You have designed for me. I know this is going to take the greatest concentration, so please help me to focus on Your plan and to refuse to allow anything to pull me away from reaching Your goal for my life! I pray this in Jesus' name!

My Confession for Today

I confess that I will achieve what God has planned for my life. I am fiercely determined to keep pressing ahead, and I will never stop until every part of my God-given assignment has been fulfilled. I have set my sights on reaching God's plan—and I will not stop until I can confidently say, "I've done exactly what Jesus wanted me to do!" I declare this by faith in Jesus' name!

Questions for You to Consider

1. Do you know what God has called you to do with your life? Are you really confident of your calling, or are you just taking a stab in the dark, hoping you are headed in the right direction?

2. If you keep pursuing God's plan at the rate you are moving at right now, will you reach your God-ordained destination?

3. What changes do you need to make in order for you to reach the goal God has planned for your life? Why not make a list of ten things you need to do to streamline your life and help you stay more focused so you can successfully do what God has called you to do?

Day 9

What Lies in Your Future if You Choose to Give Up and Quit?

> *Now the just shall live by faith: but if any man draw back, my soul shall have no pleasure in him. But we are not of them who draw back unto perdition....*
>
> —Hebrews 10:38-39

One day, as I was ministering in a certain church, the pastor of the church asked me if I would take the time to have lunch with a minister who had previously been associated with many great men and women of faith. The pastor told me that this minister had worked at one time on the staff of a very large and successful ministry. However, after deciding that his assignment there was finished, the man had left to start his own ministry.

Several years had passed since this particular minister had taken the step of faith to start his own organization. But because his new organization hadn't grown as quickly as he had wished, he had become very discouraged and depressed. As a result of these disappointments, he had begun to question everything he believed about walking by faith. He had even become very bitter and sour toward anyone who claimed to walk in faith. Unfortunately, this minister made the mistake of starting to measure what he believed by what he was experiencing.

That day when I went to lunch with this man, I was shocked that anyone who had known such a high level of faith could slip into such a miserable state. He wasn't just negative; he was extremely critical and cynical of anything that had to do with faith. As I tried to encourage this man, he said, "Yeah, I know all about you faith guys! Name it and claim it; that's who you guys are! But you're all so shallow. You guys don't know anything about hardships or suffering. You just live in a fairy-tale world that doesn't touch anyone's real existence."

As this man alleged that I and my other faith friends didn't know anything about hardships, I thought of all the personal challenges I had been through — the many assaults the devil had made against my life and my ministry. I also thought about how the very ministries he was specifically accusing of being shallow had stood so steadfastly against problems of which he was obviously unaware.

I felt a need to speak up and tell the man about some of these challenges and how I and my fellow ministers had won the victory by standing steadfastly in faith. But when I tried to speak to him, it was like talking to a concrete wall. He had already made up his mind that God had no plan of victory for his life — and that anyone who believed it was God's will for people to be victorious was a charlatan!

After two hours of this man's verbal abuse, I told the pastor who brought me to the lunch, "Excuse me, but I am not going to sit here and be verbally abused by this man anymore. I don't even know him, yet he is viciously attacking me and my friends. I'm sorry he wouldn't listen to me today, because I believe I could have helped him."

With that, I pushed away from the table, stood up, put on my jacket, and left the restaurant. There was no reason for me to stay there any longer, because the bitterness in this man had defiled him so completely that he wasn't willing to hear anything from me or from my friends who also believe in the walk of faith. In the end, I discovered the only reason he wanted to meet me for lunch was to have the opportunity to berate me for what I believed.

That experience made me think of Hebrews 10:38 and 39, which says, "Now the just shall live by faith: but if any man draw back, my soul shall have no pleasure in him. But we are not of them who draw back unto perdition...." These verses tell us explicitly what happens to people who walk away from the life of faith. According to this verse, the ramifications of this departure from faith are grim and ghastly. The man who berated me that day at lunch was a perfect example of what this verse communicates to you and me.

The words "draw back" are from the Greek word *hupostello*, which is a compound of the words *hupo* and *stello*. The word *hupo* in this case means "back," and the word *stello* means "to send." But when these two words become the word *hupostello*, it depicts someone who is "shrinking back, withdrawing, retreating, regressing, receding, backing away, backsliding," or someone who is "recoiling" from something. This is a person who started on a journey but then abruptly reversed his direction. He is now moving backward instead of forward. For some reason, this person is backing out of a position or belief that he once strongly held.

The word "perdition" is the Greek word *apoleia*, which describes "something so ruined and rotten that it is decomposing," such as rotten potatoes that have sat too long and are now spoiled and ruined. Frequently this word was used to describe *the stench of a decaying animal or a dead human body* — a loathsome, putrid, vulgar, disgusting, nauseating scent. One whiff leaves you with a sick feeling in the pit of your stomach. The smell is so repulsive that you feel like running to the bathroom to vomit. This is exactly the image that Hebrews 10:39 gives us of what happens when a person turns and walks away from the call of God or a life of faith. It results in a sickening, stinking situation.

Don't be like the man given in this example above. If God has spoken to you, stand fast and refuse to budge until you receive the manifestation of the promise God made to you!

I am amazed at the short-lived nature of some people's faith. For example, if their prayers for healing aren't answered as quickly as they wish, they permit their flesh to lead them to the conclusion that it must be God's will for them to be sick! Or if they sow their finances believing for a financial harvest but don't see that harvest after a few months, they conclude that what they were taught about prosperity must be wrong.

But you have to give faith time to work! Faith and patience are partners. That is why Hebrews 10:36 says, "For ye have need of patience, that, after ye have done the will of God, ye might receive the promise." The word "patience" comes from the word *hupomene*, a compound of the words *hupo* and *meno*. The word *meno* is the primary root of the word, and it means "to stay, to remain, to continue," or "to permanently abide in one place." It is the very word that Jesus used in John 15:7, when he said, "If ye abide in me, and my words abide in you, ye shall ask what ye will, and it shall be done unto you." A literal translation of John 15:7 could be, "If you steadfastly and continuously abide in Me, and if My words steadfastly and continuously abide in you, you may ask what you will, and it shall be done for you." The word *meno* gives the idea of something that is "rooted, unmoving, and stable."

But when you add the prefix *hupo* to the front of *meno*, thus forming *hupomene*, the picture changes radically! In this situation, the word *hupo* means "under," as to be underneath something that is very heavy. But when it is connected to the word *meno*—becoming the word *hupomene*—it pictures "a person who is under a very heavy load but who has resolved that he isn't moving"; he is going to stay in that one spot. Regardless of how heavy the load or how long it takes, he refuses to move from his position because he knows that it is where he is supposed to be!

The word *hupomene* pictures a person who is completely committed to maintaining his position. He will stay under that heavy load as long as it is necessary for him to achieve his victory. He is intent on standing by his commitment, regardless of the cost he must pay. Nothing can sway or move him to change his mind. He is not going to relinquish his territory! One scholar says *hupomene* would be better translated "endurance" because it portrays "an attitude that never gives up." It is a faith that manifests as a tough, resistant, persistent, obstinate, stubborn, tenacious spirit that refuses to let go of what it wants or believes. I personally translate the word *hupomene* as "hang-in-there-power"!

You must have *hupomene* if you intend to beat the devil at his game and successfully do what God has called you to do. If *hupomene* is working in your life, it's just a matter of time until your victory comes to you. It's not a question of if your victory will come — it's only a question of when it will come. But for you to reach that glorious and long-awaited place of victory, it is essential that you have *hupomene* in your life!

So don't let loose of your faith! The day your vision dies is the day your joy will disappear, your life will be depressing, and you will turn bitter. You'll end up in "perdition" if you let go of the word of truth God gave you. You'll start putting out the putrid stench of a faith turned sour—just like that minister who backed away from his once-strong position of faith and became bitter and cynical about anyone who walked in faith. Instead of resisting the lies the devil was speaking to him and maintaining his rock-solid stance on the Word of God, he relinquished his position of faith and gave place to doubt and unbelief.

Seated before me that day was a man who had turned around and backed out of the life of faith he had once embraced. His whole mind was doused in defeat. He had even rationalized his defeat by immersing himself in a doctrinal system designed to support his depressing existence. The entire conversation with him just made me feel ill. It was sickening to see someone who once walked in victory now walking in such a terrible low-level existence.

That's why Hebrews 10:38 says, "...if any man draw back, my soul shall have no pleasure in him." It isn't a pleasurable experience to see someone who once made such advances later take a turn for the worse. In fact, it's heartbreaking.

Perhaps you know people who once intensely longed to do the will of God and who firmly believed in what God had called them to do. But when it didn't turn out the way they expected or when they hit a few unexpected bumps along the way, they said, "Forget this faith thing! It doesn't work!" Did those same people then turn around and back away from what God had called them to do or from what He had revealed to them? Isn't it sad to see what happens to people like this—people who had so much potential and who could have achieved so much if they had just held on a little longer?

Perhaps you are the one who once tried to do God's will but then allowed yourself to become discouraged and defeated. Did you throw in the towel and let the devil have his way in ruining your dream? Did you give up, turn back, and withdraw from doing what you were called to be or to do? If the answer is yes, you're probably disgusted with yourself, and you feel unhappy and unfulfilled. Right?

Well, there's no reason for you to remain in this miserable condition for the rest of your life. The table is prepared, and the meal is cooked. God is waiting for you to pull up your chair to the table, pick up your knife and fork, and begin again to dig into the awesome plan He has for your life. Don't let discouragement keep you from being who God wants you to be. Just hold fast, hold tight, and determine that you're not going to stop until you see your dream come to pass!

Aches and pains will soon be forgotten when the powers of hell move out of the way, and your dream becomes a reality. When that happens, you'll be so glad you didn't take the low road and join the club of quitters!

My Prayer for Today

Lord, I am asking You to help me stay focused and to remain determined to stay in my race of faith until I reach the finish line and receive my long-awaited prize! When the devil tries to dissuade me from holding on to my faith, help me to rebuke him, to command him to be silent, and to order him to leave! With Your Spirit empowering me, I know I will be able to keep believing and walking by faith until I finally see the manifestation of my dreams! I pray this in Jesus' name!

My Confession for Today

I confess that regardless of how heavy the load or how long it takes, I am going to refuse to move from my faith position until I achieve the victory Jesus promises to me. I will remain steadfast in my commitment, and nothing can sway or move me to change my mind. I refuse to relinquish any of my God-promised territory! My faith is tough, resistant, persistent, obstinate, and stubborn. My spirit is so tenacious that it refuses to let go! It isn't a question of IF my victory will come—it's only a question of WHEN it will come! I declare this by faith in Jesus' name!

Questions for You to Consider

1. Have you ever known people who once walked in faith but then let discouragement turn them sour? Are those individuals now bitter, hard-hearted, and cynical toward anyone or anything that symbolizes the faith they once possessed?

____

____

____

____

____

____

2. How would you describe the current status in life of these individuals after having left behind their faith and their dreams? Have their lives become better, or have they deteriorated into a sad shadow of the faith-filled lives they once lived?

____

____

____

____

____

____

3. If you have been feeling tempted to get discouraged and to give up on the dream God has given you, what steps can you take to begin to renew your hope and strengthen your resolve to hold on to the end?

Day 10

When God Hooked My Heart!

But when it pleased God, who separated me from my mother's womb, and called me by his grace, to reveal his Son in me, that I might preach him among the heathen; immediately I conferred not with flesh and blood.

— Galatians 1:15-16

I know it sounds fantastic to believe, but the first time I ever saw a Russian Bible, I was instantly able to phonetically read it. I didn't understand what I was reading, but phonetically, I could pronounce the words and read them out loud. As you may already know, I had studied classical Greek at the university level, but I didn't realize the vast similarities between Greek and Russian. The two written languages are so close that I could phonetically read Russian the first time I picked up a Russian Bible.

I'll never forget that moment. I was a speaker at a missions' conference, and as I waited for my turn to speak, I noticed a Bible sitting on the pew next to me. I wondered whose it was, so I picked it up — and when I began flipping through its pages, I understood it was a Russian Bible. But as I looked at it, I realized that I could phonetically read the words. I was literally mesmerized by the fact that I was reading Russian! When the service was over and my time of ministering was finished, I quickly rushed to the front row, picked up that Russian Bible, and "borrowed" it for a night so I could keep looking at it. I didn't know to whom it belonged, but I took it home and read it for hours, planning to return it to the exact same spot where I had "borrowed" it that morning.

That night in my hotel room, I spent hours flipping through the pages of that Russian Bible. Slowly, I pronounced the words, fairly certain that I was accurately pronouncing what I was looking at. God knows I have a love for languages — and that night, God hooked my heart with the Russian language in a Russian Bible. The next morning, I returned that Russian Bible to the exact place where I had found it. But that experience ignited a desire in me to learn the Russian language — and that is really what started my love for the Russian language and people!

I searched for a system of learning the Russian language, and I found one that suited me very well. Every night before I went to bed, I began to memorize Russian words and study Russian grammar. I would practice my new words and phrases on Denise — all the while not understanding why I was so driven to learn this language. In just a short time, I had committed to memory 800 Russian words and could speak key phrases and sentences. Something inside me was calling out for me to learn this language.

Not long after I started studying Russian, I received a phone call from a dear friend, who invited me to join him and a few other men who were going to teach in the first aboveground Bible school established in the Soviet Union for more than 70 years. At first, I didn't want to go, but the idea of practicing Russian in real life had hooked my heart, and I found myself agreeing to join them on the trip. Within a matter of weeks, I was in the USSR, and to my delight, I spoke and understood some Russian without mistakes. That stoked the coals of the fire ignited in my heart on the night I started flipping through that Russian Bible, making me want to understand and speak the Russian language even better.

In Russia, I found myself in a land completely different from our own in the United States, but I supernaturally fell in love with the people, the culture, and even the inconveniences that existed at that time. It was like a spirit of adventure had been loosed inside me. It was, without question, a life-transforming moment in my life. But this divine adventure all started the night I "borrowed" the Russian Bible at the mission conference some months before. That I could immediately phonetically read the Russian language was a miracle to me!

Prior to this revelation, I had always assumed that my life and ministry would be based in the United States, and I never dreamed of ministering in Russia. But I learned that God has deep-laid plans for our lives that are usually revealed to us one step at a time.

This experience makes me think of the apostle Paul, who was perfectly trained to minister to Hebrew-speaking people, yet God sovereignly called him and separated him to minister to the heathen nations of the world. Although he was unaware of it, it had always been a part of the plan of God for his life.

Paul referred to this in Galatians 1:15 and 16, where he said, "But when it pleased God, who separated me from my mother's womb, and called me by his grace, to reveal his Son in me, that I might preach him among the heathen; immediately I conferred not with flesh and blood."

According to Paul, God had a plan for him from his birth, and that grace carried him toward his life call even when he was unaware of it. God "separated" him from his mother's womb for a purpose. The word "separated" is from the Greek word *aphoridzo*, which means "to mark off, to set boundaries around," or "to specifically set aside" and thus dedicate for a special purpose. Although Paul was ignorant of it, God had already marked his life and dedicated it for a ministry to the Gentiles. Heaven's plan was set in motion by grace and ultimately led him to his place of divine destination.

Paul went on to say in verse 16, "To reveal his Son in me, that I might preach him among the heathen; immediately I conferred not with flesh and blood." Paul uniquely understood that although his entire life had trained him to minister to Hebrew-speaking people, God's hand was on his life to point him in a different direction: to minister the Gospel of Jesus Christ to the heathen. The Gentile world was totally different from the world Paul knew and felt comfortable in, yet it was his place of divine purpose. When he realized it, Paul said that he "immediately did not confer with flesh and blood...."

The word "immediately" is important because it tells us that when Paul first realized God's call on his life, he didn't confer with flesh and blood. A time came later when he sought the counsel and friendship of Jewish leaders who would affirm his ministry. But initially, he simply embraced the call before the Lord with all of his heart. The word "conferred" is the Greek word *prosanatithimi*, and it refers to "obtaining favor or approval from others to endorse one's activities." Paul knew so strongly that he was called to the Gentile world that he didn't need or seek the approval of others. This calling was seared into his soul.

Likewise, when I knew that God was calling me to the Russian-speaking people, I really knew it. I did seek the counsel of others out of respect for them. However, their answers wouldn't have swayed me from my decision, because I inwardly knew that God was moving our family to the former USSR to impart the teaching of God's Word at a crucial moment in the history of Christianity in that part of the world. I heard God's call, and I accepted it. I knew that He had marked my life off, set His boundaries around me, and specifically dedicated me for this place of service.

For me, it all started with my picking up that Russian Bible — God used that incident to hook my heart with a love for the Russian language. As I think about my journey from that moment to this present day, I am in awe of God and His ways. How lovingly He works to hook our hearts and get us on the right path for our lives!

In what ways has God hooked your heart to get you pointed in the right direction for your life? You are not here by accident. God has a plan for your life. He separated you from your mother's womb to fulfill that assignment. If you don't know that yet, ask the Holy Spirit to begin to open your eyes to see why you are here and what you are to do with your life. Your life will begin to take on real purpose only when you know what you are supposed to do and you begin to follow that plan.

Like the apostle Paul, God's plan may be different from what you had anticipated. But keep your heart open to Him, knowing that God only has good plans in store for you and that He wants your life to make an impact for eternity!

My Prayer for Today

Father, I thank You for the plan for my life that is already written by Your hand deep within me. I realize that Your plan may be different from what I've previously assumed. So I choose now, as an act of my will, to lay aside my own preferences. I make a conscious decision right now that my will is to do Your will. Set my feet upon the path of Your perfect plan for me. Holy Spirit, help me not to frustrate the grace of God, but to be open-minded so I can hear You speak to me. And give me the courage to obey what I hear. I know that You have marked off my life and set boundaries around me, preparing me for a special purpose. Help me have open ears and an open heart so I can hear and understand and follow exactly what Your plan is for me. I pray this in Jesus' name!

My Confession for Today

I confess that according to Ephesians 2:10, Jesus Christ has a predetermined purpose for my life, and His grace is carrying me toward that divine destination. I will not follow the voice of a stranger, but I will follow the voice of my Good Shepherd as He leads and guides me on the path to the center of His will for my life. I am so thankful that God's grace is at work in me. I fully trust in this work of grace, and I declare that because of it, I will always be right on time and right where God wants me to be — doing precisely what He has asked me to do and thus fulfilling His will for my life. I declare this by faith in Jesus' name!

Questions for You to Consider

1. Can you think of other Bible characters who were called out of their comfort zones to minister to people who were different from them? Who are some of those people? What can you learn by meditating on their lives and experiences as they followed God's plan?

2. Do you personally know people, like myself, who thought they knew the will of God, only to find out later that He had a different plan? Who are some of those people? What happened as a result of their redirecting the course of their lives to follow God's plan?

3. What do you believe God is calling you to do right now? Is there anything that has hooked your heart and God has used as a "lure" to lead you in a new direction? Pay attention when God hooks your heart, for this may be the way He is revealing the correct path for your life to you.

Day 11

What Kind of a Special Vessel Are You?

> *But in a great house there are not only vessels of gold and silver, but also of wood and earth....*
>
> — 2 Timothy 2:20

There are many different roles in God's Kingdom, and each role is significant and important. The devil often tells people that their role is not important because it is less visible than the roles of others. Let me address that misconception by first telling you about an experience I had many years ago in an antique store that specialized in ancient relics.

When I looked at the shelves of the antique store, I was amazed at the many antiquities that appeared to have been sitting there for decades and were covered with a thick film of dust. An archeologist's treasure trove, this shop was also a housekeeper's nightmare because it hadn't been cleaned in years! I sneezed as I accidentally breathed in dust while rubbing my hand across the front of a beautiful vase I had taken from a high shelf.

From where I was standing, it appeared to me that the higher shelves were loaded with interesting historical items, such as vases of marble, jasper, and alabaster. I grabbed a stepladder and stretched upward on my toes so I could peer deeper into the cache of relics on that top shelf — and there I discovered genuine Roman antiquities made of silver and gold. Astonishment is the only word I know to describe the intense emotion that rushed through me as I reached out to take hold of those precious artifacts.

The lower shelves were also filled with memories from the ancient world, but these were primarily items made from stone and clay. I saw pottery from the Iron Age, oil lamps from the Byzantine period that had been dug from the soil of Israel, and authentic pottery from the ancient city of Corinth that was still completely intact.

As I stood back and looked at the floor all around me, I could see that I was surrounded by less expensive ancient items that were primarily made from wood, such as an ancient harness used for oxen, feeding troughs, and Egyptian baskets of woven ancient reeds from the Nile River. The thought hit me strongly that whether these different objects were made of superior or relatively inferior material, they had all successfully endured the test of time and survived thousands of years.

I pondered all these objects for a moment, wondering:

- Who had owned these objects?
- How had they been originally used?
- Who were the wealthy people who owned the gold and silver objects?

- How had the precious items been originally displayed in the palaces of the rich?

When I picked up the items made of wood and clay, I could still see stains that remained from ancient times. I wondered:

- Who had used these wooden and clay utensils?
- Had they been a part of a kitchen?
- Were they originally used in some type of workroom?
- Were some of these ancient items once used in someone's barn?

Before me were vessels of gold, silver, stone, wood, and clay, all of which had survived the test of time and now sat in that shop as a reminder of a people from the ancient past. The rich, the poor, the upper class, the lower class, the educated, the uneducated, old, and young — all the various classes of society were represented in the array of utensils and articles before me that day.

When I saw this amazing mixture of gold, silver, wood, and earthen vessels, my thoughts went to Paul's words to Timothy, where he told the younger minister, "But in a great house there are not only vessels of gold and silver, but also of wood and earth: and some to honor, and some to dishonor" (2 Timothy 2:20).

I want you to notice that Paul began this verse by writing about "a great house." At this point, Paul reached into the secular world and borrowed an example to make his point. In his mind, he recalled the magnificent homes that belonged to the rich upper class. When he wrote about a "great" house, he used the word *megale*. The word *megale* depicts "something very large." The word "house" is *oikos,* the regular word for "a house." But when the words *oikos megale* are used together, it no longer refers to just a regular residence or house like any citizen would live in. Now it paints the picture of a "very large house."

Remnants of large, elegant residences from Paul's day are still evident today in cities like Rome, Athens, Pompeii, and ancient Ephesus. Such homes belonged to the wealthy upper class and were both splendid and grandiose. Paul used the illustration of these impressive houses to depict the majesty of God's house, which is the grandest and greatest of them all.

Paul went on to say that just as in the large homes of the wealthy, in God's house, "...There are not only vessels of gold and silver, but also of wood and earth...."

The word "vessels" is the Greek word *skeuos*. It refers to "a vessel, a container," or "a utensil." In ancient times, there was a wide array of *skeuos*, and each had a specific and designated purpose. The word *skeuos* could be used to depict utensils, agricultural instruments, baggage, equipment of various sorts, vases used in worship, kitchen items, and elegant articles of gold and silver put on public display.

Vessels made from "wood and earth" were usually functional items used for everyday household chores. The wooden items were also used as containers for water, flour, oil, or wine. Vessels fashioned from "gold and silver" were evidently intended for exhibition and therefore displayed in visible places in the homes of the rich. Gold and silver objects were meant to be seen and appreciated rather than serve a practical function.

There is no doubt that Paul was describing real gold and silver vessels, because he used the word *chrusos*, the Greek word for "gold," and the word *arguros*, the Greek word for "silver." The Greek word for "wood" is *zulina*, which describes "any vessel made of wood." The word "earth" is the Greek word *ostrakinos*, which refers to "pottery." What a variety of vessels we see in this verse!

With this example, Paul teaches us that all kinds of vessels and people are needed in God's house. Imagine how dysfunctional a house would be if all the vessels in it were made of gold, silver, precious stones, or highly priced porcelain. You couldn't function in such a house! In fact, you would probably be afraid to even move about in a house where everything was made of precious materials. For a house to function normally, it needs regular pots and pans. The utensils in the kitchen may not receive the same adulation as the more elegant objects displayed in the living room showcase, but kitchen utensils are indispensable for the proper functioning of a household. Just try cooking bacon and eggs in porcelain vases or with utensils made of gold and silver, and you'll be quickly reminded how important regular ol' pots and pans are!

By using such imagery, Paul let us know that all kinds of vessels — people with different functions and roles — are needed in God's house. Although they are different from each other, each is important and special. Each serves a specific purpose. Just as was true with the vessels of the fabulous ancient homes, in God's house, there must be many different kinds of people with different positions, functions, and purposes. In fact, His house is filled to overflowing with human vessels whose various gifts and talents are essential to the effective functioning of God's house. Some people have visible positions; other people have less visible positions. But each person is vital to the operations of God's house.

As you ponder your own role in God's house, it is important for you to remember that some people's roles are more visible, while others have a less visible part to play. Yet everyone's role is vital and of great consequence. If those working behind the scenes didn't do their part, those with more visible roles wouldn't be able to do their parts.

Human beings tend to glamorize people who perform on the stage, but entertainers wouldn't seem so glamorous if they had no makeup artists to prepare them. They wouldn't shine so brightly if there were no lighting specialists to light up the stage. Their voices would be unheard if there were no sound technicians. The makeup artists, lighting specialists, and sound technicians are unseen, but I guarantee you that their absence would be noticed if they didn't do their jobs! They are all vital for the show to go on!

So don't let the devil badger you into thinking your role is not important because it is less visible than others. Your part is very important in God's house!

There are many different roles in God's Kingdom, and each role is significant and important. Maybe your role is visible, or maybe yours is behind the scenes. Regardless of the role you have right now, consider it an honor that God would use you in His house! I encourage you to say yes to the role God has given you at this time. Throw open your arms, embrace it, and hold it close. Take deep into your heart the place of service to which God has assigned you for this season. Master that position — fulfilling its responsibilities with an excellent attitude — and then watch Him move you to higher levels of responsibility according to His will and His purposes for your life!

My Prayer for Today

Father, I thank You for speaking to me so strongly today about my role in Your House. I admit that in the past, there have been times when I was tempted to think that I was less important than others because my role wasn't as visible as theirs. But now I understand that my part in Your house is just as vital as those who are more public, for without my role, it would be much harder for them to do what You have called them to do. I ask You to give me grace to embrace, hold close, and take deep into my heart the position You have given me at this time in my life. Help me master it and fulfill my part in a way that is helpful to others and that honors and glorifies You. I pray this in Jesus' name!

My Confession for Today

I confess that I am thankful for the role I have in God's house. I am not a complainer or one who bemoans the task that has been given to me. I fulfill my role with a happy heart, as unto the Lord, knowing that I will answer to Him for the assignment He has given me. Because I do my part, others are able to do their part. We are a team, and each of us is very important to the proper functioning of God's household. I appreciate my role; I value those who have different roles than mine; and I am known as a person who expresses my gratitude to others for what they do in God's house. I declare this by faith in Jesus' name!

Questions for You to Consider

1. Have you ever been frustrated with the task that has been given to you in God's house? Did you think your role was less important than others' tasks because yours was only a supportive role? After reading today's *Sparkling Gem,* how has your attitude changed toward the supportive role you have been given?

2. Can you think of someone you know who is infected with "star sickness" and who treats others badly if they don't hold a prominent position? What have you learned by observing this person's inappropriate treatment of other people? Through observation, what have you learned that you never want to do to other people who have less visible roles than yourself?

3. Has the Holy Spirit spoken to you today about embracing your place in God's house? What changes do you need to make in your attitude to be successful in your present role in His Kingdom?

Day 12

"Welcome to Your New Home!"

As they ministered to the Lord, and fasted, the Holy Ghost said, Separate me Barnabas and Saul for the work whereunto I have called them.

— Acts 13:2

When I made my first missions trip to the USSR, it was in the spring of 1991, just months before the Soviet Union finally dissolved. I was shocked by how dilapidated everything seemed to be. From what I observed, the mighty USSR was worn out and falling apart. The streets, sidewalks, cars, shops, people's clothing — everything I saw — simply looked either broken, exhausted, or worn out.

I checked into my hotel, and when I pulled the curtains back to give me a view of the street below, they were so rotten that they ripped right off the curtain rod into my hands. For the rest of my stay there, I had no curtains. There was a dead mouse in one corner of the room, and the shower looked like it hadn't been cleaned in decades. I was simply stunned that a global superpower that had kept the rest of the world in fear for so many years was so utterly dilapidated.

The next morning after our arrival, my teammates and I walked to the building where the first above-ground Bible school was being conducted — the first in more than 70 years. Two hundred and twenty students had gathered from every republic of the USSR to attend the school, and I wept when I realized this was a dream come true for them. They lifted their hands to worship, and the Spirit of God moved across the large classroom in a powerful manner. His presence was so strong.

When I stood in front of that room full of young people from all over the Soviet Union to teach them for the first time, I approached the lectern to begin my first teaching session, opened my Bible, took a step back, and looked up at the room full of students eagerly looking back at me. And at that moment, I vividly heard the Holy Spirit speak loudly to my heart and say, "WELCOME TO YOUR NEW HOME!"

I know the voice of the Holy Spirit, and there was no doubt in my heart or mind that it was the Spirit who had spoken these words to me. Feeling shocked by what I'd just heard, I choked up and stumbled with my words a bit. Then the Holy Spirit spoke it a second time: "WELCOME TO YOUR NEW HOME!"

With that, I knew God was calling me to relocate my family to the Soviet Union. As I looked at those 220 students and the dilapidated surroundings all around me, I kept thinking, *God is calling me to make THIS my home and to embrace these students and the USSR for me and my family's future.*

Later that day in prayer, the Lord continued speaking to my spirit. He explained, "There are many good Bible teachers in the United States, but I need skilled Bible teachers HERE to undergird the massive move of My Spirit that is happening. That is why I am calling you to move here and to do it as quickly as possible."

This was completely contrary to the plans I had made for my life and ministry. Back in those days, we were receiving 900 invitations a year to come and hold seminars in churches and speak at conferences. The growth of our ministry was literally exploding in the United States — and my books were becoming bestsellers. I had never dreamed of moving away from America and leaving that life behind. But that was exactly what God was calling us to do. That week, as I ministered every day to the students, the love of God in me connected me to them, and I could begin to visually see our family living in the USSR.

When I came back to Tulsa after that missions trip, I knew I needed to break the news to Denise. I didn't know how she would respond, but the Lord had prepared her heart before I ever said a word, and the same grace that was upon me was upon Denise. She said, "I'm not excited yet, but when we step onto that plane to move, I'll be filled with faith and anticipation." Our sons were too young to understand what the Soviet Union was, so they just exploded with glee that we were going to be doing something adventurous as we followed the will of God.

Finally, the morning came when Denise and I and our three small sons gathered at the airport with family and friends. We hugged and kissed everyone and told them all farewell; then we stepped onto the plane that would carry us to our new home in the former Soviet Union. As we sat down in those seats on the plane, Denise and I looked at each other with jubilation, because we knew we had passed a major test. We had said yes to the Lord, surrendering to His revealed will for us, and we were on our way to the greatest adventure of our lives.

Saying yes to the Lord requires surrender. I'm talking about that moment when you are willing to lay down all your own plans and yield to what the Holy

Spirit has revealed to you about God's will for your life. Some people pass this test, whereas others do not. However, those who surrender, yield, and obey experience the joy, power, and victory of the Spirit. They live an enriched life filled both with opportunities to be seized and obstacles to be overcome in order to attain victory and to complete the assignment.

I want to tell you how I felt that day when the Holy Spirit said, "WELCOME TO YOUR NEW HOME!" It immediately reminded me of Acts 13:2, which says, "As they [the elders in Antioch] ministered to the Lord, and fasted, the Holy Ghost said, Separate me Barnabas and Saul for the work whereunto I have called them."

Barnabas and Saul had been serving in the church of Antioch for several years when suddenly during a time of prayer and fasting, the Holy Spirit said, "Separate me Barnabas and Saul for the work whereunto I have called them." The word "separate" is the Greek word *asphortidzo*, and it means "to mark off, to set boundaries around," or "to set apart for a special purpose." The verse continues to say that they were to be set apart "...for the work whereunto I have called them." Apparently, God had a "work" for these two men that exceeded what they had done in Antioch.

Serving in Antioch was an honor, but it was not the ultimate goal of God's call on their lives. Way beyond Antioch, Barnabas and Saul [Paul] would be used by God to touch and revolutionize the Gentile world. Had they stayed in Antioch, they would have missed the adventuresome apostolic life that God had designed for them. Accepting and obeying God's call thrust them forward into a life and ministry of divine purpose that radically affected the development and growth of the Church of Jesus Christ all over the Roman Empire.

Everything Paul and Barnabas had done in ministry until that time had been nothing more than preparation for what lay ahead. Although they had spent several serious years in ministry, it was simply "getting-ready time" for the ultimate call that was before them.

This is precisely how I felt when the Holy Spirit spoke to me about my new home. God has blessed our ministry immensely, but I was suddenly aware that everything that had occurred until that moment was preparation for what was about to follow. And what was about to transpire was so immense that it made everything up to that moment look minuscule. Those previous days were days of proving to learn how to be faithful. God was watching — and now that He was satisfied, He was ready to launch us into the calling He had for our lives, which was far larger than anything that Denise or I had imagined or anticipated.

Barnabas and Saul were immediately sent forth to begin their apostolic ministries, but it took me several months to really embrace what God had said. However, I did come around, and our family entered the greatest phase of our lives as a result. We have never had any regrets about leaving America behind and moving to the former USSR.

Today, I want to encourage you to let the Lord reveal to you His plan for your life. It may be different from what you had previously thought. It is possible that everything you have done up until now has merely been preparation for a greater call before you. So open your heart and be careful to pay heed if the Holy Spirit affirms that He's leading you to take a new direction. It could add more fruitfulness and adventure to your life than you ever dreamed possible!

My Prayer for Today

Father, I thank You for Your predetermined plan for my life — and that You want to launch me into it as soon as I'm ready. I ask You to help me prove myself faithful where I am, so I will be prepared for the call that lies ahead of me. Help me not to be stuck in my thinking — assuming that where I am is the ultimate end of what I am called to do. I ask You to open my eyes to see that great and wonderful things lie ahead of me if I will fully surrender to You! I pray this in Jesus' name!

My Confession for Today

I confess that God knows the good plans He has for me. He is ordering my steps along His ordained path, and I am following the Holy Spirit's direction to do all He is leading me to do in preparation for God's next phase of my life. I recognize now that all I have done thus far has been preparation for the next part of His call on my life. Jesus, You said if a man is faithful in little, You will put him over much. So I declare that I will be faithful in every assignment You've given to me now, and I believe that You will promote me to the next phase when You have found me proven and ready. I declare this by faith in Jesus' name!

Questions for You to Consider

1. What are you doing right now to give yourself fully to the tasks at hand, so God will know that you are proven and ready for the job ahead of you?

2. Has God ever told you something that caught you off guard and by surprise? If so, when was that, and what did He say? Have you followed through on what He spoke to your heart?

3. Are you doing what God has told you to do right now? Are you being faithful with the call that He's given you? If God were asked this question, how would He answer about you?

Day 13

The Joy Set Before Jesus!

Looking unto Jesus the author and finisher of our faith; who for the joy that was set before him endured the cross, despising the shame, and is set down at the right hand of the throne of God.

— Hebrews 12:2

When a person initiates a new, huge endeavor, his passion to succeed in that endeavor strengthens him to keep his eye on the goal in front of him. For example, as an athlete starts a race, his desire to win that race helps him keep his eyes fixed on the finish line. While constructing a building, workers who keep their eyes on the architect's finalized rendering are encouraged to sustain the momentum of the building process.

But what do you think Jesus focused on when He was hanging on the Cross and enduring the agony and shame? You can imagine that He must have had moments when He thought, *I don't have to do this! I could call on legions of angels to deliver me! I could come down from this Cross!* What do you think motivated Him to remain there until the job was done?

Hebrews 12:2 tells us very clearly: "...who for the joy that was set before him endured the cross, despising the shame, and is set down at the right hand of the throne of God."

This verse says Jesus focused on "the joy" that was set before Him as He endured the Cross. Just like a runner focuses on the finish line, like a builder forges ahead to view the completed project, and an author anticipates the last written page of a book, Jesus was looking forward to "the joy" of finishing. I'm sure that as Jesus hung on the Cross, He looked out across eons of time and saw the faces of people who would be saved because of what He was doing. He saw you, He saw me — but what else did He see that motivated Him to stay faithful to the end?

The word "joy" in Greek has a definite article, which means this wasn't just joy in general, but it was a "specific joy." What was it? The verse goes on to describe that joyous "finish line" that Jesus set His face like flint toward: "...who for the joy that was set before him endured the cross, despising the shame, and is set down at the right hand of the throne of God." Jesus had His eyes of faith fixed on the empty throne at the right hand of the Father that was reserved for Him once His victory was complete. Upon that throne, all enemies would be His footstool, and He would commence the next part of His high priestly ministry to intercede for everyone who would ever come to Him in time of need (*see* Hebrews 4:16).

Jesus had His eyes, His heart, His mind — His whole being — fixed on that highly exalted place. That was the joy set before Him. When sin and hell were defeated, and Jesus was resurrected, that was the seat of authority He ascended into Heaven to occupy. And ever since that time, from that highly exalted position, Jesus has been serving as Lord of the Church and as the High Priest and Intercessor for every believer.

What is the goal in front of you that keeps you motivated to move ahead even when things are difficult? If you have no goal, it's likely you'll give up. That's why it is so important to know exactly where you are headed, what will happen when you get there, and what kind of victory you'll experience when you attain that long-awaited position. Just as Jesus needed a joyous outcome to be set before Him, I guarantee that you need one too.

- What are you building with your life?
- What keeps you motivated to stay on track?
- What will it look like when you finish it?
- What are you "writing" with your faith?
- What will the final chapter of your life look like because you've done what Jesus has asked you to do?
- What is the specific joy that is set before you?

Sometimes when you are working hard to do what God has asked you to do, it can seem overwhelming, but progress is gained one step at a time. The increments of forward movement might seem tiny, but no matter how big or small the steps, you can know that you are inevitably progressing toward the goal that God has set for your life.

When I was a young man, God showed me the purpose of my life, and that purpose has been in front of me ever since. In times of hardship, I've kept my eyes focused on that goal, because fulfilling that divine purpose is what my life is all about. Sometimes it seemed like all I could do was take baby steps — yet each step has been a step in the right direction. That's the way I've lived my entire life, focused and moving in the direction of the purpose God has revealed to me.

If you get your eyes off the goal and start focusing on how small your steps are along the way, it is probable that you'll get discouraged and give up before you arrive. So today I want to encourage you to lift your eyes and look beyond to the joy, the victory, and the fulfillment of what God has planned for your life. Even Jesus needed a goal to help Him stay focused as He underwent intense suffering and hung on that Cross.

So today, I exhort you to make a fresh consecration before the Lord to submit to His will for your life. Then exercise your authority in Jesus' name and resist the devil (*see* James 4:7)! And as you move forward in obedience to the Lord's voice, keep your eyes of faith fixed on the prize Jesus has set before you. That is what will sustain your determination to stay in place and stay on track until you can finally shout that you've reached your God-ordained goal!

My Prayer for Today

Father, I thank You for the example of faithful endurance Jesus displayed when He suffered the pain and the shame of the Cross for me. Jesus kept His eyes fixed on the joy set before Him, knowing He would occupy His seat at the right hand of the Father reserved for Him once His victory was complete. When You raised Jesus from the dead, Father, You raised me up also to be seated in Him. Lord Jesus, I worship You, and I fasten a steady gaze on You so that I will finish my course with joy to the glory of God! I pray this in Jesus' name!

My Confession for Today

I confess that I am focused on the goal of completing God's plan for my life. I realize that I am not my own, but I belong to God. Therefore, I draw upon the mighty strength that is available to me in Christ — and by the help of His Spirit within me, I move daily with unwavering devotion in the direction toward the prize of fulfilling my divine purpose as God has revealed it to me. I declare this by faith in Jesus' name!

Questions for You to Consider

1. What has God set before you as the main project or goal for your life?

2. If you don't know the purpose for your life, have you ever asked God to show it to you? According to James 1:5, God will answer this very important question for you if you've met His conditions.

3. Can you describe what a life with purpose would look like to you? How would it change the way you are living if you knew exactly what God's purpose is for your life?

Day 14

Uncomfortable Questions That Are Healthy to Ask Yourself

Examine yourselves, whether ye be in the faith; prove your own selves....

—2 Corinthians 13:5

Second Corinthians 13:5 tells us to "examine ourselves" from time to time to see if we are in the faith. This is especially true as we witness the direction society is going in these last of the last days.

That word "examine" is the Greek word *peiradzo*, which actually refers to "an intense examination." This could include a test by fire, a test based on questions, or a test that includes some type of self-examination. A test of self-examination is the most pain-free option, even if you must ask yourself questions that require answers that are uncomfortable to confront.

So today, why don't you do a little self-examining and see how well you fare? Open your heart, be honest, and talk to yourself and to God about these questions. They are designed only to help you consider possible areas where you may need to change.

What do you give to God financially?

Since actions speak louder than words, take a look at your financial giving and see what it reveals about whom you love most. Do you give the tithe, as commanded by Scripture, or do you regularly make excuses for not giving and use the money elsewhere for personal pleasures or other things?

If you are honest today, what would you say that your giving reveals about your love for God?

What do you do with your time?

Do you make spending time with God a top priority in your life? Or do you complain that you do not have time to pray or read the Bible, yet you somehow make lots of time to visit with friends, watch television, go to the movies, and do other things that you want to do?

If God Himself looked at your life and measured what you love most by the things you dedicate your time to, what would He say?

What do you do to serve others?

It's amazing how many people claim to love God, but never have time to serve Him in a practical way in a local church. Words are easily spoken, but actions prove a person's sincerity.

By looking at your life, would God say that your actions prove you are more devoted to your own needs and interests, or that your life demonstrates you are in love with God's Church?

When you pray, what do you pray about? Do you pray about yourself only, or do you pray for the needs and dreams of others?

It is easy to think of your own needs and desires, but how often do you focus your prayers on the concerns of others? When you pray, does God hear you primarily praying for yourself, or does God hear you praying for other people, too?

If God were to give a report about the things He hears you pray about, would He report that you are an unselfish person who is concerned about the needs and dreams of others, or would He report that you are concerned only about yourself and your own needs?

What personal sacrifices do you make to serve the Lord?

How long has it been since you gave something up or changed your schedule to help someone else or to walk in obedience to God's plan? Can you honestly say that you are picking up your cross and dying to your own interests in order to serve others and to make a difference in someone else's life?

If God opened the books to reveal the sacrifices you have made for Him or others, would the record reveal that you care deeply for God and live in obedience to His commands, or would it show that you are unwilling to inconvenience your life in any way or sacrifice any of your private plans?

What do your spending habits reveal about you?

When you look at the money you spend on your hobbies, personal possessions, and other non-essentials, and then compare it to the amount of money you invest in the Gospel, what does it reveal about your love for God and concern for others who need to hear the saving message of Jesus Christ? We can all mislead ourselves to think we are generous, but if God Himself gave His view of what your spending habits reveal about your priorities, what would He say about you?

Would God say the Gospel is most important to you, or would He say that your spending habits reveal that your driving motivation in life is simply pursuing comfort and pleasure?

What are you sacrificing to be obedient to God?

Is there anything you are laying down in order to walk in obedience to God and His Word, or would you have to honestly say that you don't sacrifice much for God or others? Are you willing to be inconvenienced to help someone else or to serve in the church, or are you unwilling to jeopardize your own comforts and pleasures?

Would God say your life reveals that you are willing to pick up your cross to do what God asks of you, or that you do everything you can to avoid letting anyone or anything inconvenience you?

What does your lifestyle reveal about your priorities?

Does your daily lifestyle reveal that you love entertainment, pleasure, comfort, and happiness the most? Are you consumed with yourself and your own needs and offer no service to anyone else if it requires you to sacrifice your time, energy, or comfort? Or can you honestly say that you are living your life primarily for Jesus, fulfilling His plan for you in these last days?

If God were to comment on your lifestyle, would He say that it is dedicated to Him and to fulfilling His plan? Would your priorities match those of a selfish or unselfish lifestyle?

A day is coming when the truth about you will be known! The secrets of the heart will be made manifest, and the truth will be laid bare before God. So wouldn't it be much wiser for you to let God deal with your heart now — to expose those areas of your life and thinking that need to be changed so you can be more conformed to the mind of Christ?

If you let the Holy Spirit deal with you now and bring about the necessary changes in your life, you will be able to confidently and joyfully look into the eyes of Jesus on that day you stand before Him. And you will be known as one who loved Him most of all in these last days when so many were caught up with being "lovers of pleasure more than lovers of God" (2 Timothy 3:4)!

My Prayer for Today

Father, I come before You now as humbly as I know how, and I ask You to shine the light of Your Word into every hidden place of my heart to reveal my true motives to me. Disobedience produces self-deception, and Father, I realize that actions speak far louder than words. I have often praised You with my lips, yet my heart was far from You as I rationalized and justified my self-seeking priorities with self-deluded excuses for being a lover of self more than a lover of God. Holy Spirit, I ask You to help me judge myself and lay aside every weight and sin that can so easily trip me up. More than anything, I desire to please You, Father, and to honor the Lord Jesus who gave His life for me. Today, like Jesus, I choose Your will above my own. I yield all I am and all I possess to You for Your exclusive use. I am not my own. I belong to You. I have been bought with a price, the precious blood of Jesus Christ. Therefore, I yield to Your transforming power more than ever before. On the day I stand before You and the books of my life are opened and read, I will receive a crown to set at Your feet, just as I lay my life before You now. I pray this in Jesus' name!

My Confession for Today

I declare that I examine myself in the light of God's Word and I apply what the Holy Spirit reveals. I refuse to delude myself with reasoning that is contrary to truth. I choose to be a doer and not merely a hearer who listens to the Word but refuses to internalize its meaning or to act on the truth. I respond to wisdom's voice, and I bring my life into alignment with God's purposes and plan. I choose to agree with God; therefore, I walk in harmony with His will and His ways. I don't waste my life. I keep my focus on Jesus and on eternity. On that great day when I stand before Him, my reward will be that in this life, I was fruitful for His glory because I obeyed. I declare this by faith in Jesus' name!

Questions for You to Consider

1. Did the questions in this *Sparkling Gem* stir you to self-examination and repentance, or did they provoke anger? If anger, why did they make you angry?

2. Did the Holy Spirit actually cause you to pause on one or more of these questions to reflect more deeply on what it was asking? If so, which question in this self-examination really stood out to you?

3. What area(s) do you feel the Holy Spirit is speaking to you about that you need to address and change? We each have areas that we need to work on, but just between you and God, which areas are you convicted about?

Day 15

A Fight Always Follows Illumination

> *But call to remembrance the former days, in which, after ye were illuminated, ye endured a great fight of afflictions....*
>
> — Hebrews 10:32

Have you ever received a word from the Lord that gave you the exact direction you needed? If so, let me guess what happened next. Suddenly — BOOM! It seemed like all hell broke loose! The craziest circumstances erupted, seeming to directly challenge and assault that word you had just received from God!

If I've just described what you've gone through or what you are going through right now, be encouraged! You must be right on track! A spiritual fight usually does occur when you've been specially illuminated to the plan God has for your life.

In Hebrews 10:32, the Bible says, "But call to remembrance the former days, in which, after ye were illuminated, ye endured a great fight of afflictions...." Today, I want us to look at three key words in this verse: "great," "fight," and "afflictions." These words describe what you and I might experience after the Lord has given us a word of instruction to illuminate us regarding His plan for our lives.

First, let's look at the word "great." In Greek, it's the word *polus*, and it means "a huge number" or "to an enormous degree." By using this word *polus*, the writer of Hebrews tells us that sometimes spiritual conflicts accompany a word of divine direction, and they are normally not challenges of little consequence that can be easily overcome with minimal effort. In fact, the enemy's attacks are usually *polus!* In other words, they're significant attacks — the kind of trials that require all of your determination to hold fast and not give up!

The second word I want you to see is the word "fight." It comes from the Greek word *athlesis* and refers to "a committed athlete." This undoubtedly tells you that when you receive a word from the Lord, it may throw you into one of the greatest challenges of your entire life! You'll feel like you've just entered the ring and are competing for the prize!

Finally, we come to the third word, "afflictions." It is the Greek word *pathema* and usually refers to "mental pressure" or to "suffering that affects the mind." This isn't talking about mental sickness; rather, it points to a war in your soul or an attack on your mind.

Hebrews 10:32 could thus be taken to mean:

> *"After you were illuminated, you endured an enormous ordeal that threw you into the biggest fight you ever faced in your life. But the most critical part of the struggle resulted from the unremitting assaults that literally battered your mind...."*

You can be sure that if you take a stance of faith in response to a word you received from God, every possible negative thought will come against your mind. Not only will the devil try to use people and circumstances to thwart the plan, but he will also affect your mind with all kinds of negative thoughts and accusations. He'll do everything he can to talk you out of doing what God has called you to do.

Don't be surprised by this! You must remember that Jesus experienced this type of attack as He hung on the Cross. As He selflessly laid down His own life on the Cross, the soldiers and other criminals hurled their horrible, slanderous statements at Him. But Jesus pushed aside all the assaults that came against His soul and endured, committing His life and destiny into the Father's hands.

So if you have received a word from God for your life, let me ask you:

- Did you go through a huge ordeal yourself after you were illuminated to God's plan?
- Did you feel you were thrown into a fight that came to challenge what God had told you?
- Did you find that the devil tried to assault your mind and emotions with lies, accusations, and fears?

If you have been in this place I'm talking about — or if this is exactly where you are right now — then be encouraged! This is probably your clearest signal that you've received a real word from the Lord. You must be right on track, because the devil is terribly concerned about what will happen if you act on what God has revealed to you.

Don't back down. Don't surrender to the enemy's vicious lies in your mind, his attacks against your body, his challenges to your finances, or his assaults on your relationships. Regardless of how much resistance he tries to bring against you, don't you dare back up on that word God gave you!

If you hadn't received a true word from the Lord, there would be nothing for the devil to challenge! The fight you face is the greatest evidence you're right on track! Just hang on, and don't give up! You're clearly headed in the right direction!

My Prayer for Today

Lord, as I take a stand of faith in response to that word I have received from You for my life, I realize that Satan may try to use negative thoughts to war against my mind. Thank You for alerting me to the fact that the devil may even try to use people and circumstances to thwart Your plan for my life. But I also thank You that Satan cannot stop Your plan from coming to pass! With Your Spirit illuminating my mind, I know I will be able to discern the attacks of the enemy and successfully resist each and every attack! I pray this in Jesus' name!

My Confession for Today

I boldly declare that I won't back down! I won't surrender to Satan's vicious lies — his attacks against my body, his challenges to my finances, and his assaults against my relationships. Regardless of how much resistance he tries to bring against me, I will not back down on the word that God gave me. I will stand fast, holding tightly to what God has promised, and the devil will be the one to throw in the towel and surrender! I will resist him until he flees and leaves me! I declare this by faith in Jesus' name!

Questions for You to Consider

1. What are some past instances when you received direction for your life that you knew was from God?

____

____

____

____

____

____

2. Were you bombarded with negative thoughts and pressures that tried to make you doubt the direction God gave you? How did you react?

____

____

____

____

____

____

3. In the future, how can you respond according to the Word when these negative thoughts and pressures come against God's direction for your life?

Day 16

Are You Tired of Waiting for Your Fruit-Producing Season?

> *Rooted and built up in him, and stablished in the faith, as ye have been taught, abounding therein with thanksgiving.*
>
> — Colossians 2:7

Have you ever been so frustrated at waiting for a fruitful time in your life that you said to the Lord, "When is the fruit-producing season ever going to start in my life? I've worked, believed, and waited, but I am a little tired of waiting to see the fruit I long to see in my life. How long do I have to wait, Lord?"

I encourage you today to stay on track and refuse to give up, because you're about to reach the greatest period of fruitfulness you've ever known. Before a fruit-producing tree reaches a time in its growth when it blossoms and bears fruit, first it sends its roots down deep into the earth, where it can draw on a constant source of nourishment. Then, as it continues to be nourished from below, it begins to send its limbs upward and outward.

During the life of that tree, it must endure the elements of every season — the heat, the cold, the sleet, the rain, and the snow — before it ever blossoms. Because those roots are deeply tapped into a continuous source of strength, nourishment, and energy, the tree is able to outlast all the seasons and eventually become a fruit-producing tree.

Psalm 1:3 uses the example of a tree to declare that when a person is rooted in God's Word, he is "...like a tree planted by the rivers of water, that bringeth forth his fruit in his season; his leaf also shall not wither; and whatsoever he doeth shall prosper."

If you are wondering how long it is going to take before your fruit-producing season finally arrives, don't get too discouraged! The bigger the tree, the greater the need for that tree to send its roots down deep into the earth to draw nourishment and to give it a firm footing against the wind, the weather, and the elements of the different seasons. That continual nourishment will also protect the tree from pestilence that may try to attack it through the years.

In light of this, consider what the apostle Paul wrote in Colossians 2:7: "Rooted and built up in him, and stablished in the faith, as ye have been taught, abounding therein with thanksgiving." I want you to especially notice the word "rooted" in this verse. It comes from the Greek word *ridzo*, which means "to be firmly and deeply rooted," making the object "fixed, steady, stable, and strong." This is the picture of a strong tree whose roots go down deep and reach its source of nourishment. The tree is also held securely in place by those roots, regardless of the weather or the environmental opposition that comes against it.

Rather than complain that it's taking too long for your fruit-producing season to arrive, you need to thank God for this time in your life! Take this time to send your roots down deep and tap into the strength of God's Word and God's Spirit. If your roots are securely fixed in Jesus Christ, you will outlast every season, every foul climate, and every storm. Eventually, you will enter into the finest fruit-producing season of your life, your ministry, your family, or your business.

Honestly, you need to thank God that things haven't happened faster in your life! Have you ever seen someone who reached success too quickly? That person usually loses his success just as quickly as he gained it because he didn't have the roots and the experience necessary to maintain the success he gained. When people achieve success too quickly, it often means they don't have the roots, the depth, and the sure foundation to bear them up in the difficult times they will encounter as they go through the seasons of life.

So take this time to work on your personal life, your mind, your thinking, your discipline, your finances, your weight, your relationships, and your behavior. While you are waiting for that fruit-producing season to come to pass in your life, use this time to put off the old man and to put on the new man (Colossians 3:9,10). Spend this phase of your life wisely by renewing your mind to the Word of God (Ephesians 4:23) and being certain your affections are set on things above, not on things of this earth (Colossians 3:2).

If you use your time wisely, there will be no wasted time in your life. But if you just sit around and complain that it's taking too long to get where you want to go, you will waste time. Sitting and complaining doesn't make anything happen faster — and it often further delays the manifestation of the answer you've been waiting for.

So refuse to belong to those who are grumpy and complaining all the time. Instead, look at this time in your life as a blessing sent from Heaven to help you get yourself rooted deeply in Jesus Christ! Then send your limbs upward and outward as you tap into the power of God. Eventually, you'll begin to see blossoms budding in your life, signaling that you are about to enter your long-awaited season of bringing forth much fruit!

My Prayer for Today

Lord, I thank You for not sending success to me too quickly. I know that if I had achieved success earlier, I wouldn't have been ready for it. In fact, I might have destroyed it due to my own lack of experience and my immaturity. Help me embrace this time in my life as a time of preparation. Help me to truthfully analyze every part of my life in order to see what areas need to be more deeply rooted in You. I want my roots to go down so deeply that no storms of life and no attacks from the devil will be able to move me from the place where You have called me. Help me to stay so fixed, firm, strong, and stable that once I enter the fruit-producing season, I will never leave it! I pray this in Jesus' name!

My Confession for Today

I confess that I am firmly and deeply rooted in God's Word. As a result, I am fixed, steady, stable, and strong like a tree whose roots go down deep. I am tapped into the life of Jesus Christ, and He has become my Source of nourishment. I am held so securely in place that I am unaffected by the storms of life and the pestilence that the devil tries to use to attack me. I will outlast every season, every foul climate, and every storm. I am about to enter into the finest fruit-producing season of my life, my ministry, my family, and my business. My fruit-producing season is getting ready to begin! I declare this by faith in Jesus' name!

Questions for You to Consider

1. Have you ever seen people quickly reach success, but it seemed that they lost their success just as quickly as they attained it? Can you name specific individuals who come to mind as examples?

2. What were the reasons these individuals gained and lost success so quickly? Reflect on this question for a while; then write down your observations.

3. What do you need to be doing differently in your own life to make sure you don't ever fall into the category of those who quickly gained and quickly lost success?

Day 17

The Essential Attitude for Success!

Let a man so account of us, as of the ministers of Christ, and stewards of the mysteries of God.

—1 Corinthians 4:1

We live in a world that loves to take it easy. We want instant results — and we want them right now. Technology has made almost everything instantly accessible. Our entire Western lifestyle is centered around making things as easy, fast, effortless, and painless as possible.

The younger generation is so accustomed to getting everything they want that they don't understand there is a price to pay for true success. But whether they like it or not, the fact remains: True greatness, great achievements, and real success won't float to them on clouds that suddenly materialize above their heads. If anyone wants to achieve something great and significant, he or she will have to put a lot of hard work and effort into making it happen.

Let's take the apostle Paul as an example. I recently read a report that made this claim: Apart from Jesus Christ, the apostle Paul more dramatically affected Western civilization than any other man in human history. Paul achieved incredible feats in his life. His epistles have impacted world history and leaders, and what he accomplished in his life and ministry remains legendary. So let's look at this famous Christian leader and ask:

- How did Paul live his life?
- What kind of attitude did he possess regarding his life mission?
- What attitude did he possess that enabled him to dramatically affect his world?

In First Corinthians 4:1, Paul wrote, "Let a man so account of us, as of the ministers of Christ, and stewards of the mysteries of God." I believe that some very important answers to the questions above are found in this interesting statement that Paul himself wrote.

In this verse, Paul calls himself a "minister." This is the Greek word *huperetas*, a vivid term that conveys "the essential attitude necessary to get a job done"—especially the work of the ministry. However, this word doesn't apply only to ministry. It also denotes the essential attitude a person must possess to become successful in any sphere of life.

Interestingly, this word *huperetas*, translated "ministers" here, was used in classical Greek society to describe "low-class criminals." The first time I studied this Greek word, it seemed so odd that Paul would use this word to describe himself and his attitude toward the ministry. I wondered:

- Why would Paul use such a word?
- Is he using this word as a picture to make a point to us?

After a lot of digging into the original Greek, I found out exactly why Paul used this word. He was a successful man who understood what it took to get a job done — and no word more vividly explains this work ethic than the Greek word *huperetas*.

Originally this word described the very lowest class of criminals. These criminals were so low, so detestable, and so contemptible that they were outcasts and removed from society. Often they were assigned to the bottom galleys of huge shipping vessels, where they literally became the engines of those huge ships.

And the harsh assignment given to these criminals wasn't temporary either. They were sentenced to live the rest of their lives in the darkness below the deck — endlessly rowing, rowing, and rowing. Their entire existence was devoted to keeping that ship moving toward its ultimate destination! These *huperetas* were officially called "under-rowers" because they lived and rowed down in the bottom of the ship. Day after day, their job was to heave those massive oars forward and backward, pushing them through the water to make the ship move through the sea.

This is the same word the apostle Paul uses to describe the attitude that is necessary to do what God has called us to do! God has called us to take our place in His plan — to grab hold of an oar, so to speak, and begin to serve Him practically in some way. We are to keep rowing, rowing, rowing, and rowing, doing our part and fulfilling what He has asked us to do.

Some people tend to sit and watch as achievers reach out to do the impossible. But if you are going to join the ranks of those achievers, you'll have to do more than just sit around and talk about it. You'll need to say yes to what the Lord is urging you to do.

And remember, these *huperetas* who rowed the boat didn't quickly finish their assignment of rowing; it was their responsibility for a lifetime. In the same way, we need to realize that the secret dream God has put in our hearts probably won't be achieved quickly either. It may be an assignment that will last for the rest of our lives. It takes hard work and a lifelong commitment for us to achieve the great things that God wants to do through you and me!

I heartily recommend that you mentally prepare yourself for a long-term stint at doing what God is calling you to do. It will almost certainly take unbelievable strength and energy to move that vision from the realm of dreams to the realm of reality. So jump into the bottom of the boat; take your place on the rowers' bench; and begin to row with all your might! With each step of obedience you take and each day of faithfulness you live, you will come closer to the desired destination — the ultimate fulfillment of God's plans and purposes for your life.

We may live in a world that loves to take it easy and that delights in instant results. But in order to achieve the true greatness God desires for us, we will have to be determined, committed, and willing to do anything necessary to accomplish what He has for us.

No, real success doesn't float to you on clouds that suddenly materialize above your head. Therefore, I encourage you to make the decision to start putting a lot of hard work and effort into making your assignment successful. It's going to take every ounce of strength you have to make your dream come to pass, so you might as well resolve to get started today!

My Prayer for Today

Lord, I am determining in my heart today to jump into the bottom of the boat, grab an oar, and start rowing with all my might. Doing the minimum is never going to get me where I need to go, so right now I am making the choice to put all my energies forward to achieve what You have planned for me. Help me to be faithful, steadfast, unmoving, and unflinching in the face of opposition. Help me to tell my flesh to be silent when it tries to scream out that I'm doing too much! I choose to crucify the flesh and press forward with all the strength You give me. As I do this, I believe that You will make my dreams come to pass! I pray this in Jesus' name!

My Confession for Today

I confess that I will see the fulfillment of the dream God has put in my heart. I am a hard worker, willing to do whatever it takes, and I have made a long-term commitment to achieve all that God wants to do through me! It will almost certainly take unbelievable strength and energy to move that vision from the realm of dreams to the realm of reality, but I can do all things through Christ who strengthens me! With God's Spirit working in me, I will see the fulfillment of my dreams! I declare this by faith in Jesus' name!

Questions for You to Consider

1. If you keep operating at your current level of production, will you reach the goals God has given for your life?

2. Be honest! Has your desire to have things "easy" been a hindrance to you? Has your desire for "creature comforts" overpowered your desire to reach your goal regardless of the price you must pay or how long it takes?

3. If you continue at your present momentum, will you dramatically affect your world and environment as the apostle Paul affected his? If not, what changes do you need to make in your thinking to become a great achiever?

Day 18

You Are One of God's Pillars!

> *Therefore, my beloved brethren, be ye stedfast, unmoveable, always abounding in the work of the Lord....*
>
> — 1 Corinthians 15:58

Have you ever looked at someone and thought, *Wow, that person is such a rock!* What does it mean to you when you think of someone as a "rock"? That's a strong statement, so it would be well worth your time to think it through and decide what characteristic makes a person a "rock" to you, to someone else, or to a church, business, or organization. Even more importantly, would others call you a "rock"?

In First Corinthians 15:58, Paul writes, "Therefore, my beloved brethren, be ye stedfast, unmoveable, always abounding in the work of the Lord...." I want you to look at the word "stedfast" in this verse, because it illustrates what kind of person God considers to be a "rock" in His family.

What does it mean to be steadfast? This word "steadfast" is the Greek word *edraios*, which has several meanings:

- It means "to be stationary," such as something that sits in one place for a long, long time.
- It describes "something that is firm and steady."
- It was frequently used in connection with *foundations or support structures in buildings.*
- It portrays something that is "strong, unbendable, unbreakable, and permanent," such as a well-built foundation for a large building or a strong column that holds up a roof.

So when Paul urges us to be "steadfast," he's calling on us to be totally reliable — not shaky or undependable. We should be stationary in the roles God has called us to fulfill in the Body of Christ. We shouldn't be quickly shaken or easily lured to some other place or some other task. We must be like pillars, foundations, or supports in the house of God.

When you take the Greek word *edraios* into consideration, it means First Corinthians 15:58 could be interpreted: "...Be reliable; dependable; not easily excited, shaken, or affected...."

What is the purpose of a huge stone pillar in a building? Its purpose is to support the roof or some other important section of the building, correct? What would happen if you suddenly jerked that pillar out of its place? You'd find out very quickly that the pillar had been essential to holding up the place! Remove that pillar, and the entire building would collapse into a heap of rubble, creating a horrible, terrible mess!

When God tells you to be "steadfast," He is asking you to be a "rock" in His house — like a pillar that faithfully stands in its place and helps to hold things together. He wants you to be so dependable that people lean on you, counting on the fact that you'll always be there to help keep things together. And when events occur that shake up everyone's world a bit, God wants people to look to you as one who isn't easily excited, shaken, or affected.

Now that you know the kind of "rock" God needs you to be, would you say that you qualify to be called a "rock" today? Would others call you a "rock," or would they say you are up again, down again, easily excited, and not too dependable? If you got really honest with yourself, would you judge yourself to be steady, sturdy, and reliable — or unpredictable and undependable?

Don't view yourself as small, insignificant, or unimportant. God needs you, and other people are depending on you. It's time for you to realize that God meant for you to be part of the foundation of the Body of Christ! You can be a "rock" in His family and a person on whom others can lean and depend.

If you're thinking differently from this, you need to change your thinking. Instead of focusing on how insignificant you are in God's great plan for these last days, start focusing on becoming steadfast, immovable, and always abounding in the work the Lord has assigned to you!

My Prayer for Today

Lord, I want to be the person You and others can depend on. Forgive me for any instability in my life, and help me overcome every weakness in my character. Just as I have looked for others to be "rocks" in my life, I want to be a "rock" to other people. I have a lot of room for development in my life, but I am willing to be changed. I want to be taught, corrected, and taken to a higher level. Today I ask You to do whatever is necessary to make me the strong and reliable kind of person You want me to be! Please do Your special work inside me! I pray this in Jesus' name!

My Confession for Today

I confess that God's Word overcomes the weaknesses in my personality and character. God calls me to be "steadfast" — and I AM steadfast. God and people see me like a pillar that stands in its place and helps to hold things together. I am so dependable that people can lean on me, counting on the fact that I will always be there to help keep things together. When events occur that shake up the world around me, I am not easily excited, shaken, or affected. Praise God, I am becoming more and more dependable all the time! When people hear my name, they think of someone on whom they can rely! I declare this by faith in Jesus' name!

Questions for You to Consider

1. Can you think of five people who have been "rocks" in your life? Why not go out of your way to let those people know how much you appreciate them?

2. What strengths did those people exhibit that made you think so highly of them?

3. Is there anyone who needs your strength right now? What can you do to be a "rock" to that person in his time of need?

Day 19

You Are No Accident, Because God Chose You!

> *According as he hath chosen us in him before the foundation of the world, that we should be holy and without blame before him in love.*
>
> — Ephesians 1:4

From time to time, someone says, "My parents didn't plan me. I was an accident no one expected." People use this as an excuse for not accepting more responsibility in life, claiming that they are accidents who came into the world by mistake and aren't even supposed to be here!

Well, I want to tell you that even though we may have been a surprise to our parents, we were not a surprise to God! The Bible teaches that long before you or I were ever conceived in our mothers' wombs, God already knew us and was calling us to be His children with a special purpose to fulfill in this world.

In Psalm 139:15 and 16, David declares that God's eyes were fixed on us not only when we were in the earliest stages of being formed in our mother's womb, but even before we were conceived. David said concerning himself (and us), "My substance was not hid from thee, when I was made in secret, and curiously wrought in the lowest parts of the earth. Thine eyes did see my substance, yet being unperfect; and in thy book all my members were written, which in continuance were fashioned, when as yet there was none of them."

According to David, God knew us when we were nothing more than mere "substance" in the earliest stages of being formed in our mothers' wombs. God was so intricately aware of us that He took note as our arms, hands, fingers, legs, feet, and toes were being formed. In fact, this verse says He even knew us "...when as yet there was none of them" in existence! Think of it! Long before we were conceived, God already knew of us — and by faith He could see us being conceived, formed, and born into this world. This means there isn't a single human being on the earth who was a surprise to God, and that includes you!

Those of us who are believers were also saved by no accident. Paul writes, "According as he hath chosen us in him before the foundation of the world...." The word "chosen" in Greek is *eklego*, a compound of the words *ek* and *lego*. The word *ek* means *out,* and the word *lego* means "I say." Together, these words literally mean *Out, I say!* It can also mean "to call out, to select, to elect," or "to personally choose."

In classical Greek writings, this word *eklego* referred to "a person or a group of people who were selected for a specific purpose." For example, the word *eklego* was used for the selection of men for military service. It was also used to denote soldiers who were chosen out of the entire military to go on a special mission or to do a special task. Finally, it was used for politicians who were elected by the general public to hold a public position or to execute a special job on behalf of the community.

In every case where the word *eklego* is used to portray the election or selection of individuals, it conveys the idea of the great privilege and honor of being chosen. It also strongly speaks of the responsibility placed on those who are chosen to walk, act, and live in a way that is honorable to their calling. Because of the great privilege of being elected to a higher position or selected to perform a special task, those who are "chosen" bear a responsibility to walk and act in accordance with the calling that has been extended to them. They should look upon themselves as chosen, honored, esteemed, and respected — special representatives of the one who elected them!

So when Paul says that God "...hath chosen us in him before the foundation of the world...," he is saying that God looked out to the horizon of human history — and He saw us! And when God saw us, His voice echoed forth from Heaven: "Out, I say!" In that flash, our destinies were divinely sealed! We were separated by God from a lost and dying world, and He called us to be His own.

Just as the word *eklego* in classical Greek times depicted the military selection of young men to leave their homes and come serve in the military, God looked out at the human race and personally selected, elected, and specially chose us to come away from the world and be permanently enlisted as His sons and daughters! Now as children of the King, we bear the awesome responsibility of walking worthily of the high calling we have received!

Look at when this selection took place. Paul says it occurred "...before the foundation of the world...." The word "foundation" is the Greek word *katabole*, a compound of the words *kata* and *bole*. The word *kata* means *down*, and the word *bole* means "to hurl" or "to throw." These two words together mean to forcibly hurl something down, and it refers to the act of creation.

Thus, before God ever spoke the earth into existence — before His booming voice ever called out for the first layers of the earth's crust to be put into place — He had already spoken our names! He selected and elected us before the very first layers of the earth were created.

In light of these Greek meanings, Ephesians 1:4 could be phrased to read: "When God saw us, He said, 'Out, I say!' In that moment, He separated us from the rest of the world and enlisted us in His service. And think of it! He did all of this before He ever hurled the first layers of the earth's crust into existence...."

So if your flesh ever tries to rant and rave that you're not worthy enough to be used or that you're just an accident, you need to take authority over your flesh and tell it to shut its stupid mouth! Then you need to declare, "God chose me, and He planned a great future for me. He wants to use me. I'm not going to listen anymore to this foul garbage from my lying flesh and unrenewed emotions. I have an awesome destiny! In fact, I'm a significant part of God's plan!"

Don't listen to your filthy, stinking, lying, fibbing flesh anymore! God has been waiting for your arrival for a very long time! It's time for you to accept His assignment and make the necessary changes to flow with His program. He's calling out to you all the time, saying, "Get up and jump in the race! I want you. I'm calling you to be part of My team."

There is too much at stake for you to make the mistake of sitting around and feeling sorry for yourself. You'll only begin to experience true significance when you accept the fact that God has chosen you, and when you begin to live up to the glorious calling He has placed on your life! No matter how large or small the task, no matter how big or tiny the assignment, joy and satisfaction will be yours when you start accomplishing what God brought you into this world to do.

This is what imparts true significance to any person's life. No satisfaction compares with this satisfaction. Those who contribute nothing to life are usually the ones who struggle with a sense of purposelessness.

Even if you think your gifts are small in comparison to others, you can still use them! If you use the gifts God gave you, they will increase. And the more proficient you become at using those gifts, the more valuable you will become to your family, your church, your business, and your friends. On the other hand, you will cause your life to be inconsequential if you ignore the gifts God gave you and minimize the life assignment He has entrusted to you.

A person's life becomes pointless when he or she contributes nothing to the world. Don't let that describe YOUR life! God didn't bring you into the world so you would live a pointless and inconsequential life! He has a purpose for your life. He wants to use you! He wants you to be a significant part of His plan!

My Prayer for Today

Lord, I am so glad that You knew me and called me even before I was conceived in my mother's womb. According to Your Word, I am no mistake; therefore, I ask You to help me start looking at my life with respect, esteem, and honor. You called me, and You have an awesome plan for my life. I ask You to help me uncover that plan so I can get started on the road of obedience toward the fulfillment of what You brought me into this world to do! I pray this in Jesus' name!

My Confession for Today

I boldly declare that I am no accident and no mistake! God knew me before the earth was created; He called me before I was formed in my mother's womb; and He has long awaited my arrival on planet earth! God has a plan for me! I am purposeful; I am respectful of myself; and I walk in a way that honors the One who called and anointed me to be enlisted in His service! I declare this by faith in Jesus' name!

Questions for You to Consider

1. Have you ever been tempted to think that your life was pointless and inconsequential? What happens in your life most often that triggers these negative emotions?

2. Can you think of a time when you were supernaturally illuminated to the call of God on your life? When that happened, what did you understand was the chief purpose that God had for you in this lifetime?

3. If you have been struggling with feelings of purposelessness or of inferiority toward other people, what are you going to do to stop these negative emotions from affecting you in an adverse way?

Day 20

You Can Make a Difference in Someone's Life!

> *And of some have compassion, making a difference.*
>
> — Jude 1:22

If you are burdened for someone who isn't serving God the way he used to, it's time for you to do something about it. Worrying won't change a thing! But turning that worry into action can make a big difference in the outcome of that other person's life.

You can make a difference in someone's life! That is precisely why Jude 22 tells us, "And of some have compassion, making a difference." Do you see the word "compassion" in this verse? This important word is taken from the Greek word *eleao*, which in this case refers to "deep-seated and unsettling emotions" a person feels when he has seen or heard something that is terribly sad or upsetting.

These are the kinds of emotions that well up inside you when you see a child whose stomach is bloated from malnutrition and starvation. You might also feel these emotions when you see a person who is emaciated and dying of terminal cancer or a destitute family that is forced to live on the streets with no food or money.

Jude's purpose in using the Greek word *eleao* is very plain. He is doing exactly what television programs do when they flash pictures of starving children with bloated stomachs on the television screen in front of us. The producers of these programs show us these kinds of worst-case-scenario pictures in order to stir us to action.

These pictures of desperate misery from Third World countries are flashed in front of us while emotionally moving music plays in the background. Then the celebrity host on the program says in an impassioned voice, "Pick up your phone and call today. Your call could save the life of a child."

These kinds of television programs are designed to stir up emotional feelings of pity. The producers of the programs realize that simply stating a need verbally would never get our attention; we're just too mentally busy in today's society. Therefore, they make the need as graphic as they possibly can, knowing that pictures speak a thousand words and are much more effective in arousing pity from our hearts.

However, arousing pity is not the ultimate aim of these programs. The horrifying pictures and emotional musical background are designed to convince you to pick up your phone, call the number on the television screen, and make a donation to help the cause of the sponsoring organization. This compulsion to act and to do something is the moment when pity is transformed into compassion. By itself, pity would simply feel sorry about the situation. But compassion cannot sit by and idly watch the scenario grow worse. Compassion reaches out to act immediately and to do something about the situation.

It is unmistakably clear that Jude wants to elicit an emotional response from his readers. He wants them to graphically see and understand the seriousness of believers who have backslidden into a life of sin and disobedience. He wants his readers to "feel" for these critically ill spiritual patients. In fact, he wants them to "feel" their condition so intensely that he says, "And of some have compassion...." In other words, Jude is telling his readers to take that pity and turn it into action!

You see, when genuine compassion begins to flow from your heart, you cannot sit idly by and simply feel sorry about a person's situation. Real compassion says, "I have to get up and do something about this!"

Because Jude uses the word "compassion," he is telling us that the spiritual condition of a backslidden believer is just as real and serious as the plight of a starving child, a dying man, or a destitute family. If you will allow the love of God to flow through you, it won't be long until compassion for these erring believers begins to flow from you to them. Then you will be compelled to see them set free from their bondage! That compulsion is the activity of compassion! You may think, "Yes, but those believers knew better! If they had stayed faithful in their walk with the Lord, they wouldn't be in the mess they are in right now. Isn't it their fault that they're in trouble?"

The answer to this question may be "Yes, they are to blame for their condition." However, consider this: Wouldn't you have compassion on a homosexual who contracted AIDS due to his own illicit sexual activity? Although his own actions got him into his mess, wouldn't it still grab hold of your heart when you saw his wasted body? Wouldn't his helpless condition make you wish there was a cure for AIDS?

In the same way, even though a sinning believer may have gotten himself into trouble because of his own actions, we must not therefore shut off the flow of God's compassion that resides within us. Believers who have become spiritually deceived need a touch of God's power more than they ever did before! Therefore, we cannot let the enemy sow hard-heartedness in our hearts toward people who have become spiritually ill or backslidden. Their plight is very serious, and they need our help and prayers of intercession!

If you know people who fit this description, it's time for you to let the supernatural compassion of Jesus Christ begin to flow out of your heart toward them. These error-ridden believers need a divine touch from God that will open their eyes and bring them back to the Lord. By releasing a flow of this powerful force toward them, you could set in motion the very deliverance these individuals need from the powers of darkness that bind their souls and keep them in deception.

This is why Jude urges us to release this delivering flow of compassion when he says, "And of some have compassion...." This kind of compassion is a mighty force that reaches even into the flames of judgment to snatch people from destruction. Why not open the bowels of your heart and allow this supernatural flow of compassion to start flowing through you today? Just think — by opening your heart and letting compassion flow through you toward these people, you could be the very one God uses to bring them back home again!

My Prayer for Today

Lord, please forgive me for being hardhearted, condemning, and judgmental toward people who have needed my prayers and intercession. Instead of wasting all my time judging them, I could have been praying for them. Now I see my mistake, and I truly repent for it. Starting today, I pledge to change my attitude — to open my heart and let the compassion of Jesus Christ flow through me to help set their deliverance in motion. Let Your compassion begin flowing through me today! I pray this in Jesus' name!

My Confession for Today

I boldly confess that compassion flows through me like a river! Condemnation and judgment have no place in my life, in my thinking, or in the way I relate to other people. I am filled with the love of God, and I allow that love to touch others who are near me. The bowels of my heart release the compassion of Jesus Christ, touching the lives of people caught in the deception of sin and darkness and setting them free! I declare this by faith in Jesus' name!

Questions for You to Consider

1. Do you know anyone who is no longer walking with God and for whom you need to be praying and interceding right now?

2. Have you acted in a judgmental way toward a sinning or erring believer — someone who really needs your prayers and intercession, not your condemnation? If your answer is yes, I suggest that you take a few minutes to get your heart right with God and then begin to regularly pray for his or her deliverance.

3. Have you ever been caught in a deception, but someone loved you through it until you were set free and put back on a straight course? Who was that person who stood with you through that ordeal? Did you ever take the time to express your gratefulness for his or her love and patience toward you during that time?

Day 21

Is it Time to Make a Change in Your Environment?

> *Wherefore seeing we also are compassed about with so great a cloud of witnesses, let us lay aside every weight, and the sin which doth so easily beset us....*
>
> — Hebrews 12:1

Your biggest potential enemy in life (besides your own wrong thinking and the devil himself) is the environment in which you live. For instance, if you constantly live in an atmosphere of doubt and unbelief, it's just a fact that you'll have a much more difficult time maintaining a walk of strong faith. That doubt-filled environment will try to rub off on you!

It's just a fact that your environment tends to affect you and the way you think. For example, if you used to smoke or if you used to have a drinking problem, it's obviously not a smart idea for you to hang around smokers or drinkers — unless, that is, you want to be influenced to return to your old habits. Hanging around people who still do these things may lure you to pick up a cigarette to take a smoke or to allow yourself one more small drink.

However, those little allowances may possibly be the very hook that the devil uses to drag you back into the bondage from which Jesus Christ already delivered you. That's why it's vital for you to understand that the environment surrounding you is very important!

With this in mind, look at the phrase "...the sin which doth so easily beset us...." What kind of sin is this verse talking about? The words "so easily beset us" are from the Greek word *euperistatos*, a compound of three words: *eu*, *peri*, and *statos*. Let's look at all three of these words.

The word *eu* usually means "well," but in this case, it carries the idea of "something that feels well" or "something that is comfortable." The Greek word *peri* means "around" or "being completely surrounded." The word *statos* is from the root word *istimi*, meaning "to stand." When these three words are compounded, the new word describes something that comfortably stands all around you, such as a comfortable environment.

So this phrase in Hebrews 12:1 could be understood to say:

> *"...Lay aside the sin and the environment that so comfortably envelops you...."*

Sometimes, in order to make necessary changes in your life, you must physically remove yourself from an unprofitable situation. If you're not strong enough in your faith to stay there without being affected, you need to get up and get out of that unbelieving, negative environment — the one you've been comfortably living in for a long, long time. If you're not strong enough to overcome it, it will unquestionably try to reach out and drag you back into your old behavior again.

If God's admonition to lay aside every weight applies to you, then obey Him and make a break from that unhealthy environment! Perhaps old friends, old places, or wrong beliefs are trying to exert a bad influence on you, and you're not resisting that influence too well. If that's the case, get out of there! For you, that environment is sin if it keeps you from fulfilling your potential in Jesus Christ.

Be honest as you consider your workplace, your friends, and your living conditions. Ask yourself, is this environment conducive to my walk in Christ, or is it dragging me back down into the mire I was delivered from?

Your friends and your job are not so important that you should let them destroy your spiritual life. If you cannot successfully handle the environment you're in, get out of there. Then watch the Lord provide a better job and better friends than you've ever had in your life!

Your Christian life is serious business. Don't let your environment fill you with doubt and knock you out of your spiritual race! If you can't handle your environment victoriously, initiate a plan of action to change it today!

My Prayer for Today

Lord, I want to stay in an environment that will keep my faith alive and strong. Help me recognize those relationships and places I should avoid to keep my faith from being negatively affected. As You show me places, people, and things I should avoid, give me the strength I need to do what is right — and give me the wisdom I need to know how to avoid those places and people! I pray this in Jesus' name!

My Confession for Today

I confess that I will physically remove myself from unprofitable situations that are not positive for my faith. I make the choice to get up and get out of unbelieving, negative environments that tend to pull me down. I am laying aside every weight, and I am making a break from all unhealthy environments! With God's help, I make the right choices and right friends. I do everything I can to stay in environments that help me keep my faith alive and well. I declare this by faith in Jesus' name!

Questions for You to Consider

1. Have you been in any relationships or environments that you should have avoided? How did they affect your walk with God?

____

____

____

____

____

____

2. Are there any unprofitable situations or relationships that you need to remove yourself from now?

____

____

____

____

____

____

3. What steps can you take to start making better choices of friends and environments? What do you think the Lord wants you to do with your current relationships and places that you frequent?

Day 22

Discerning God's Plan for Your Life

> *But as it is written, Eye hath not seen, nor ear heard, neither have entered into the heart of man, the things which God hath prepared for them that love him. But God hath revealed them unto us by his Spirit....*
>
> — 1 Corinthians 2:9-10

From time to time, we all struggle to discern the best course of action for our lives. Which decision is right? Which is wrong? What job should we take? What university should we attend? Whom should we marry? Should we pursue a secular career or go into full-time ministry? These questions are common to us all, and they go on and on and on.

In the Old Testament, knowing the will of God was truly difficult because the Holy Spirit didn't reside in people's hearts; therefore, they struggled tremendously to discover God's plan for their lives. In their efforts to uncover His will, people would seek special signs and divine signals. They'd even go visit prophets who lived in their region in an attempt to find answers and gain knowledge. God had prepared so many benefits for His people! But because the Holy Spirit didn't live in their hearts at that time, they struggled with knowing what He wanted them to do and were unable to see much of what He had provided for them or what His plan was for their lives.

However, the situation couldn't be more different today. As believers, we now have the Holy Spirit living inside our hearts — and He has come to reveal to us all the answers we need! Yet all too often, many Christians still live like people under the Old Covenant, depending on special signs, divine signals, or advice from others. Perhaps it is because they never developed their spiritual sensitivity or learned to recognize the voice of the Holy Spirit. Regardless, this should not be the case!

The Holy Spirit has come to dwell within us, and He wants to tell you and me everything we need to know!

In First Corinthians 2:9 and 10, the apostle Paul wrote to us about the Holy Spirit's ministry to reveal God's plan to us. He said, "But as it is written, Eye hath not seen, nor ear heard, neither have entered into the heart of man, the things which God hath prepared for them that love him. But God hath revealed them unto us by his Spirit...." Notice he declared that God has "revealed" His plan to us by His Spirit. The word "revealed" is a translation of the Greek word *apokalupsis*, which is a compound of the words *apo* and *kalupsis*. The word *apo* means "away," and the word *kalupsis* is the Greek word for "a veil, a curtain," or some type of "covering." When compounded, they form the word *apokalupsis*, which is normally translated in Scripture as the word "revelation." This new word literally means to remove the veil or to remove the curtain so you can see what is on the other side.

This word *apokalupsis* plainly refers to something that has been veiled or hidden for a long time and has suddenly become clear and visible to the mind or eye. It is the image of pulling the curtains out of the way so you can see what has always been just outside your window. The scene was always there for you to enjoy, but the curtains have blocked your ability to see the real picture. As soon as the curtains are drawn apart, you can suddenly see what has been hidden from your view. In that moment when you see beyond the curtain for the first time and observe what has been there all along but not evident to you — that is the picture of what the Bible calls a "revelation."

So Paul was proclaiming in this verse that when the Spirit of God came to dwell within us, one of His major missions was to remove the veil that once obstructed our view. The Holy Spirit is continually at work in us to help our eyes to see, our ears to hear, and our hearts to fully comprehend the specific, special plans that God has meticulously prepared for each one of us!

Keep this thought uppermost in your mind and heart in the days to come: The Holy Spirit — the Great Revealer — lives inside you, and He wants to reveal to you God's blessings, promises, provisions, and plans for your life! Thank God, you're not living like people did under the Old Testament. You don't have to look for special signs, divine signals, or a prophet to discern God's plan for your life.

Right inside your heart is the greatest Source of revelation on planet Earth — the Holy Spirit! If you will develop a spiritual sensitivity and learn to listen to His voice, He will reveal everything God has prepared for you so you can get on with your life and do exactly what He intricately planned for you to do!

My Prayer for Today

Father, I thank You that the Holy Spirit is a Revealer of truth. He will lead and guide me into all truth and show me things to come. I thank You that I never need to worry or even wonder about what You want me to do in any area of my life. If I ask You for wisdom and open my heart to hear, the Holy Spirit will make Your will clear to me. I praise You for Your wonderful plan and for helping me fulfill my part in it for Your glory! I pray this in Jesus' name!

My Confession for Today

I confess that the Lord guides me continually by His Spirit within me. I trust in the Lord with all my heart and don't lean to my own understanding. In all my ways, I acknowledge His wisdom and His presence, and He meticulously directs my steps to follow the good path He has prepared for me! I declare this by faith in Jesus' name!

Questions for You to Consider

1. Can you think of a specific moment when the Holy Spirit "revealed" an answer that you desperately needed to know? How did He reveal that answer to you?

2. Have you ever had a "revelation" — a moment when the Spirit of God supernaturally removed an invisible veil that obstructed your view of things — and when that view was removed, you could see everything you needed to see and know exactly what you needed to know?

3. What are you doing in your life right now that is a direct result of a special revelation from the Holy Spirit? Maybe it's more than one thing, so why not write down your thoughts and demonstrate to yourself just how much the Holy Spirit has revealed the will of God to you?

Day 23

It's Time for You to Start Using the Gifts and Talents God Has Given You!

As every man hath received the gift, even so minister the same one to another, as good stewards of the manifold grace of God.

— 1 Peter 4:10

Today I'd like to take that discussion a step further to help you get started today in activating the giftings on the inside of you on a daily basis so you can fulfill your part in God's great plan of revealing His love to man.

Here is a key to releasing your God-given grace gifts: It is something you can do on purpose. You don't have to wait around for the elusive "perfect moment."

Often, people wait and wait for the "perfect time" to launch their business, their ministry, or their big dream in life. But the truth is, very few successful people began the pursuit of their call with that kind of an ideal moment. In fact, what most people would refer to as spectacular success stories actually began very "unspectacularly." If you study the lives of individuals who have made a significant contribution to this world, you'll find that often their journey began with just a simple decision to get started.

Certainly, you can choose to wait around and wish for a "perfect moment" to come when the skies part, lightning bolts strike, and beams of glory land all around your feet to signal that your moment has arrived. But if this is what you're waiting for, I want to tell you that you will probably be waiting a very long time! That just isn't the way God does things in the vast majority of cases.

When I was a young man, I daydreamed of the time when my ministry would begin, and I could start using the gifts and talents I had received from the Lord. I would lie in bed at night and envision the day when I would finally step up to the plate and begin my ministry. Then one day, as I was praying, the Holy Spirit spoke to my heart. He told me that it was time to quit fantasizing and get started! I had always thought I was waiting for that perfect moment to take the first step. But all the while, God was waiting for me to get up and start doing something with the gifts He had placed in my life!

I knew I had a gift to teach the Bible — and since that was what God had equipped me to do, I decided to use my gift! I invited my friends to a Bible study that I would lead on the university campus where I was studying. I knocked on doors, handed out leaflets, and started to intensely prepare to teach my very first public, verse-by-verse study in the New Testament. Today, I still have the notes I prepared for the first series I ever taught, and I treasure those notes. They are memories from those early days when I was just getting started in the ministry. My beginning was small, so small it was almost unnoticeable, but it was a beginning.

Everyone has to have a beginning — including you! If you know what God has gifted you to do, don't wait around and lose precious time as you wait for a hypothetical, fantasy-like "perfect moment" to get started. Instead, why not put your hand to the plow and begin to use your gifts right now? Once you take that step of faith, God will have something to bless. But as long as you do nothing, you're not giving Him anything to prosper!

This is precisely why Peter wrote, "As every man hath received the gift, even so minister the same one to another, as good stewards of the manifold grace of God" (1 Peter 4:10). Today, I want us to look deeply into this powerful verse.

First, I want you to notice that Peter said, "As every man hath received the gift...." The words "every man" are translated from the Greek word *hekastos*, which is an all-inclusive word that literally means "every single person, no one excluded." This undeniably means that every person who has been born of the Spirit and who declares that Jesus is Lord has been supernaturally endowed with gifts from God. Because the word *hekastos* is used, it emphatically means that *no one is excluded* from these God-given gifts. Even the person with the lowest self-esteem is mightily gifted by the Spirit of God but simply unaware of the powerful gifts that reside inside him or her.

If you think that you are not gifted, you are wrong! The usage of the word *hekastos* in First Peter 4:10 clearly means that you, too, are endowed with magnificent, God-given gifts.

Peter went on to say, "As every man hath received the gift...." Pay careful attention to the word "received" in this verse. It comes from the Greek word *lambano*, which is used 258 times in the New Testament. It means "to receive into one's possession" or "to take into one's own control and ownership." It carries the idea of taking hold of something, grasping onto something, or embracing something so tightly that it becomes your very own. When used in connection with God-given gifts, as Peter uses it in this verse, it portrays God as the Giver of gifts and us as the receivers. Then, once we receive the gift of God, He sees it as our responsibility to accept and take ownership of that gift as our own.

Then Peter wrote, "As every man hath received the gift...." The word "gift" in this verse is the word *charisma*, derived from the word *charis*, the Greek word for "grace." But when the word *charis* becomes *charisma*, it speaks of "grace-given gifts." In other words, these are not gifts earned or deserved; rather, these are gifts imparted supernaturally and divinely by God's grace.

Thus, there is no room for boasting or self-glory in the possession of these magnificent gifts, for these are not natural talents developed by one's own ability. These are supernatural graces that are divinely imparted by the Spirit of God. According to this verse, God has graced every child of God with miraculous gifts that are beyond his or her own natural ability. Once released and activated, these gifts bring the life-changing power of God into manifestation to meet and answer human need.

Yes, even you have these powerful gifts inside — just waiting for you to take ownership of them and use them!

Peter continued, "As every man hath received the gift, even so minister the same one to another...." This word "minister" comes from the Greek word *diakoneo*.

This Greek word portrays "a servant whose primary responsibility is to serve food and wait on tables." It presents a picture of a "waiter or waitress who painstakingly attends to the needs, wishes, and desires of the client." It is this servant's supreme task to please clients; therefore, he serves honorably, pleasurably, and in a fashion that makes the people he waits on feel as if they are nobility. This is a committed, professional server who is fanatically dedicated to doing his job on the highest level possible.

By choosing this Greek word *diakoneo*, Peter alerted us to the fact that God expects us to be radically, passionately committed to using the gifts He has given us in such a way that pleases Him and meets the needs of others. That is why

Peter continued by saying, "As every man hath received the gift, so let him minister the same one to another...." God intends for us to use our gifts to minister to one another. These gifts are not given for self-glory or self-promotion, but for the benefit of the larger Christian community and the world around us.

What about you? Are you using your grace-given gifts to minister to the needs of those around you?

Peter concluded this verse by saying, "As every man hath received the gift, so let him minister the same one to another, as good stewards of the manifold grace of God." The word "steward" is from the Greek word *oikonomos* and was specifically used to describe "the household manager for an upper-class, wealthy home."

By using the word *oikonomos* in this verse, Peter shows us that God has indeed made us the stewards of His own personal treasures, and He expects us to give Him glory by using our gifts wisely and on time to meet the needs of those around us.

Taking all these Greek words into consideration, we could paraphrase this verse to read: "Every single one of you, without exception, has received a grace-given gift from God. Embrace what God has placed inside you. Take ownership of it, and do your best to use that special gift to meet the needs of one another. God has entrusted a lot to you by placing those special gifts in your life, and He is depending on you to be faithful with this great responsibility."

God gives you gifts and talents, and then He expects you to use them, regardless of their size. As you do, He will begin to bless the work of your hands. However, if you choose to wait for the "perfect moment" to develop before you ever do anything with your gifts, you'll probably never get started! Don't waste any more time — it's time for you to start making the most of the divine equipment inside you that's just waiting to be released!

My Prayer for Today

Lord, I want to thank You for placing spiritual gifts in my life. These gifts were given by You, and my heart's desire is to use them as You intend for them to be used. Forgive me for the time I've wasted waiting for the perfect moment before I got started. Help me now as I step out in faith to start using these gifts in ways that will benefit those around me. I know that Your gifts have power, so as I release these precious treasures, I ask that Your power will also be released to meet the needs of the people whose lives I touch. Today, I willfully recognize the gifts You have placed inside me, and I make the choice to let these gifts begin to operate through me! I pray this in Jesus' name!

My Confession for Today

I confess that God's grace works mightily in my life, and those mighty gifts have been placed in my life through this divine grace. Although in the past I have put myself down and lightly esteemed my value in the Body of Christ, I have made the decision to recognize, embrace, and take ownership of the marvelous gifts inside me! God expects me to be responsible in my stewardship of these gifts, so I will be meticulous and faithful in the way I allow these gifts to operate through me! I declare this in Jesus' name!

Questions for You to Consider

1. Do you know which gifts God has graced you with? What are those gifts that He wants to operate in your life? Have you ever made a list of the ways you believe God wants His grace to flow through your life to others? If not, it would be a good idea for you to do this so you can affirm the gifts, imparted by the grace of God, that reside in you!

2. What results have you observed from the times you allowed your God-given gifts to operate in your life? How have these gifts benefited and helped others? What impact did those gifts have on others when you allowed them to freely operate through you?

3. Can you think of people who have been waiting a long time for the "perfect moment" to come so they can get started in life? Are they still waiting?

Day 24

What Race Is God Asking You to Run?

Being confident of this very thing, that he which hath begun a good work in you will perform it until the day of Jesus Christ.

— Philippians 1:6

After years of searching for a permanent location for the Moscow Good News Church, our ministry finally found a facility that would suit our needs — that is, it would meet our needs after total reconstruction. I put the vision before our church to purchase it, and we started to believe for the funds needed to acquire it and then totally renovate it.

I likened our situation to the Israelites' divine assignment to possess the Promised Land. Just as Joshua's spies outlined the obstacles they encountered when they came back from scouting out the land, I didn't hesitate to outline the challenges that lay before our congregation. I related the facts with clarity, but like Joshua and Caleb, I made it clear that God would give us victory over every obstacle or giant along the way. The issue was not how big the giants were; the matter revolved around God's faithfulness to perform His promises and our obedience to enter into and receive the promise He had given us.

The fact is, what we were stepping out by faith to do required God's supernatural blessing because completing this mammoth vision far surpassed our natural abilities. Yet we were certain this was God's plan. Therefore, we fixed our eyes on Jesus, and we were fully convinced that He would supernaturally enable us to accomplish this mighty deed. Then we jumped in to run that race of faith. With our eyes fixed solely on the prize, we committed to do what God had asked us to do and to not stop until we had reached the finish line.

This grand undertaking required every ounce of our faith, strength, and might. It demanded the highest level of faith for finances that Denise and I had ever released in our lives. It required our concentration and our intercession. However, we knew that God had watched us for years and that He knew He could count on us, or He wouldn't have entrusted us with such a magnificent assignment.

I also knew that just as God entrusted Denise and me with the task of heading up this project, He had entrusted many faithful partners to contribute financially. God explicitly told me that people would generously help us — and that He would abundantly bless those who participated in the project. We knew the same grace that was on us would also be on our partners, and God would supernaturally grace them to supernaturally give.

The Lord assured me that unusually large gifts would be given to help Denise and me so that this huge assignment would not be a burden. Gifts and offerings would be given to help us establish this Gospel center in the heart of Russia, and Heaven would keep records of every gift given. Those gifts would be credited to people's heavenly accounts that await them there!

I have often reflected on God's faithfulness to our ministry as we ran that race of faith. He perfectly and completely fulfilled every single one of His promises to us. Although the challenges were terrific, we accomplished the vision! When we are all in Heaven one day, the fabulous building that we now occupy in Moscow will still be filled with people worshipping Jesus. From the grandstands of Heaven, Denise and I — along with all those who financially gave — will rejoice that we didn't shrink back from His command. With God's grace, we ran the race and finished it!

What race is God asking you to run in your own life? Does it seem huge, gigantic, massive, and colossal to you? When you ponder what He is asking you to do and the ramifications of your obedience, does it rattle you, shake you, or make you shudder? Does it excite you, stir you up, stimulate you, and thrill you to know that God trusts you to believe Him for the impossible?

Each one of us has come too far to shrink back from God's command now. It's too late to turn around and run the other direction. As we near the last of the last days, there's no place for fear or timidity. The time is short, and God is looking to each of us to fulfill His plan for these last generations. God is depending on you and me, and we must give our lives to do exactly what He is asking. There is nothing more important in life than heeding His voice and doing what He is requiring.

God could choose anyone, but He is choosing you. So whatever your task or assignment is, think about what an honor it is that God would use you to accomplish such a feat! You must push aside fear, reach deep inside to the anointing and power of God that resides within you, stand on His promises of provision and strength, and step forward by faith to see it done. You will never know what God can do unless you do something that gives Him the opportunity to show you!

As the children of Israel prepared to cross the Jordan River into their Promised Land, the river was at flood stage — its highest stage of the year.

Yet God commanded Joshua to instruct the priests to step right into the river! God assured him that if he did, the water would supernaturally part so that he and the priests and the rest of the Israelites could pass through on dry ground.

Imagine what Joshua must have felt. People were watching him and the priests, looking to see if the water would part as their leader had promised. Every eye in Israel was peering at Joshua in speculation. But this wasn't Joshua's moment to shrink back in fear — it was his moment to obey!

Standing on the brink of the Jordan River with its dangerous waters rising higher and higher, Joshua obeyed God's command, and the priests lifted their feet to make that first brave step into the raging, overflowing waters. As they obeyed, the waters parted just as God had promised. The Bible tells us, "And the priests that bare the ark of the covenant of the Lord stood firm on dry ground in the midst of Jordan, and all the Israelites passed over on dry ground, until all the people were passed clean over Jordan" (Joshua 3:17).

It took one man's courage and obedience for those waters to part — and because of Joshua's willingness to obey, all the Israelites passed into their land of promise. That, my friend, shows the power of one person's obedience. Your own obedience affects many lives! When you obey, it impacts many people and paves the way for others to inherit God's promises as well.

This is not to say that obedience to God is always easy or without challenges. I'm sure Joshua had to fight his thoughts, battle his emotions, and constantly refuse to give in to the trepidation that tried to flood his mind as he followed those priests into the raging river. Had Joshua listened to those thoughts and emotions that certainly assaulted his mind, he never would have obeyed. Just as you and I must do, he pushed all of it out of the way and boldly stepped out. And in the moment Joshua committed to obey, he experienced the intervening, supernatural, history-making power of God!

Those who stand on the banks and simply watch will never experience the power of God as Joshua did that day. If they want to see and experience God's power, they must be willing to get up, get out, and do exactly what God is asking them to do.

Certainly, there will be a season for you to develop a dream or vision so it can take root in your heart. However, eventually, a time will come when you must stop thinking about it and start taking action. If you don't, your dream will remain in the realm of fantasy and imagination. But when you finally act on that dream and step forward to do what God has asked of you, that is the moment you will see God move into action and part the waters before you!

I'm so thankful that Denise and I — along with our staff, our church, and our partners — put our feet into the waters in front of us. We thought, prayed, planned, and talked about it for years. Then God asked us to take action and obey. He had given us assignments in the past that we obeyed, and we had experienced His power as a result. Because of our past obedience, we were equipped and prepared by Him for the greatest step we had ever taken to that point. How could we do anything else but obey Him this time? With man it is impossible, but with God, all things are possible (*see* Mark 10:27)!

Today, this is true for you too!

- Has God given you an assignment?
- Is God asking you to start a new business?
- Has He assigned you the task of reaching your unsaved family and friends?
- Do you think God is calling you to pursue higher education?
- Is His Spirit calling you into the ministry?

Do you feel the tug of God in your heart to become a bigger financial giver?

Accomplishing what God is asking of you may seem impossible to your natural mind, but it's not impossible with Him! Whatever God is telling you to do, think it over and pray about it a lot! Then there will come a moment — maybe that moment is now — when the time of thinking and preparing must stop and action must commence. God will one day speak to your heart and say, It's time to get off the banks of the river and lift your feet to step into the waters. If you'll do what I say, I assure you that you will see My power as never before!

If you know it's time to step out in faith, you must take your eyes off the raging, turbulent waters before you and fix your eyes on Jesus Himself. He is the Author and Finisher of your faith (*see* Hebrews 12:2). You can be sure that what He starts, He will always finish. That's why Paul said, "Being confident of this very thing, that he which hath begun a good work in you will perform it until the day of Jesus Christ" (Philippians 1:6).

The word "confident" is from the Greek word *peitho*, which means to be "fully persuaded or fully convinced." Paul is literally saying, "I am fully and completely persuaded and convinced...that he which began a good work in you will perform it until the day of Jesus Christ." The word "perform" is the Greek word *epiteleoo*, which is a compound of the words *epi* and *telos*. The word *epi* gives force to the word. The word *telos* describes something that "is accomplished, culminated," or "fulfilled." However, the way it is used in Greek, it emphatically means that God Himself will move you toward the goal, and He will not stop until you have reached the end.

That means God is with you at the beginning of your journey, in the middle of your adventure, and He will empower you to make it all the way to the finish line. You may not always feel like you're an overcomer, but God's grace is moving you — one step at a time — toward your land of promise!

Joshua's obedience resulted in all of Israel passing over into their land of promise. And think how your willingness to obey will make the way clear for others to follow and to see, touch, and taste the power of God in their lives! When you obey God, it brings His power into play on a scale far greater than you could have ever dreamed or imagined. However, such power belongs only to those who obey.

- What is your life assignment?
- What is the step of faith you need to take to fulfill your own destiny?
- What promise awaits you on the other side of the river?
- What is stopping you from taking the next steps to get there?
- Is it time for you to stop just thinking and start acting on what God has given you to do?

Denise and I know what it means to accept a faith assignment; therefore, we understand what you may be feeling as you step out in faith to obey what God has told you to do. We assure you that God will protect you and supernaturally provide everything you need to accomplish the job He is asking you to do.

As Denise and I lifted our feet and stepped forward by faith to do this seemingly impossible task, we understood that it was our assignment and that God had long been preparing us for this moment. He was depending on us to obey. He is likewise depending on you to hear His voice and to do what He is telling you to do right now.

What race is God calling you to run? What river is He calling you to pass over? I deeply believe that God will empower you to do the most radical, supernatural thing you have ever done in your life. It may seem as impossible as crossing the Jordan at flood stage, but His grace and power will pick you up and carry you toward the goal, and He'll bring you all the way to completion!

If that describes you, and if you do exactly as God instructs you to do, your obedience will "split open" the Spirit realm and bring the supernatural power of God into your life on many levels. I'm convinced that your obedience will trigger miracles in your own life and in your family, relationships, health, finances, and business — including the fulfillment of things you've sought, prayed for, and desired to come to pass for many years.

So I must ask you — what do you hear the Spirit of God asking you to do? Whatever it is, your obedience will result in a manifold blessing of His power to increase you in every area of your life and to make you a blessing to many others for generations to come!

My Prayer for Today

Father, I hear You beckoning me to step forward by faith, and I am inspired to do what You are telling me to do. I've been in a preparation season for a long time. I thank You that You are finally telling me it is time to step forward, to put my feet into the river's waters and to see Your supernatural power make a way for me to enter into the land You promised to me and that You've been speaking to me about. Thank You for having confidence in me. With the Holy Spirit living inside of me, the two of us together can challenge the impossible and do the unthinkable! By faith, I am stepping forward — and I thank You for carrying me toward the finish line and helping me complete what You have put into my heart! I pray this in Jesus' name!

My Confession for Today

I declare that the impossible is moving out of the way for me. God has been preparing me for a long time to do more than I've been doing. He has tested me, watched me, prepared me, and now it's time for me to take the big leap of faith and move forward toward the goal He's put in my heart. It's a miracle, but He is carrying me toward the finish line, and He will make sure I get all the way to the conclusion. I give God all the praise and glory, for He prepares me, empowers me, and carries me toward that place He has ordained for me to be! I declare this by faith in Jesus' name!

Questions for You to Consider

1. What impossible goals have you accomplished by the grace of God? As you look back over your life and think of the things you've done, what are those things that you never could have done on your own? Why don't you take time to make a list and then thank God for His fulfilling power working in your life?

2. What are the goals that are still directly ahead of you? Have you jumped into the race and decided that you're going to pass over the raging waters that stand before you? Or are you struggling with the desire to shrink back in fear and timidity?

3. Can you think of a single instance when God has not been faithful to you? Why don't you take a few minutes to meditate on all the times God has taken you from where you were to where you needed to be?

Day 25

How Badly Do You Want to Win Your Race?

> *Know ye not that they which run in a race run all, but only one receiveth the prize? So run, that ye may obtain.*
>
> — 1 Corinthians 9:24

When runners run in a race, they have one thing foremost in their mind — the finish line! It was with this thought in mind that the apostle Paul wrote and told the Corinthians, "Know ye not that they which run in a race run all, but only one receiveth the prize? So run, that ye may obtain" (1 Corinthians 9:24).

The word "run" is the Greek word *trecho*, which means "to run" and indicates "a constant and continuous pace." This word *trecho* often depicted runners who ran a foot race in a huge stadium before crowds of adoring fans. In order for the runner to run successfully and finish triumphantly, every ounce of his strength and his complete attention were required. Paul had this example in mind as he wrote this verse.

Just as it takes full concentration and a stride that is paced for a runner to run a long distance, Paul now uses the word *trecho* to tell us that if we are going to run our race as God expects, it will require 100 percent of our attention and will mandate that we learn how to run at a constant and continuous pace. In other words, we can't try today, stop tomorrow, and then give it another shot a week later. We must be constant and consistent. Once we are in the race, we must run ferociously. On the other hand, to stay in the race on a long-term basis, we must learn to pace ourselves so we can stay consistent and avoid wearing ourselves out!

Paul tells us that we are to run until we "obtain." The word "obtain" is the Greek word *katalambano*, which is a compound of the words *kata* and *lambano*. The word *kata* describes something that is coming *downward,* and the word *lambano* means "to take or seize something." When compounded together into one word, it becomes *katalambano* — a very powerful word indeed!

For example, the word *katalambano* can picture someone who has found something he has searched for his entire life. Rather than lose it or pass up the opportunity to possess it, he pounces on it with all his might, latching hold of it and seizing it with joy! Or once again, this word can portray a runner who runs fiercely, using every last ounce of his energy as he strains forward toward the finish line. At last he reaches the goal and crosses the finish line. The prize is now his! He won the reward because he put his whole heart, soul, and body into obtaining it!

In light of the words *trecho* and *katalambano* found in this verse, First Corinthians 9:24 carries this idea:

"Don't you know that those who compete in a foot race run with all their might and strength against the other runners, but only one wins the competition and takes the prize? In light of this, run with all the might you can muster! Go the distance, and pace yourself to make sure you have enough energy to get to the finish line, where you will finally latch hold of and possess that which you have been so passionately pursuing!"

At the end of Paul's own life, he wrote, "I have finished my course" (2 Timothy 4:7). He triumphantly exclaimed that he had done it! His race was finished! He had given his spiritual race all he had to give; he had run with all the might he could muster; and he had run so consistently over the years that he had finished a winner! All those years of being concentrated and focused finally paid off! If Paul had approached his race with an attitude of lazy complacency, the prize would have gone to another. But because he had "run to obtain," he obtained!

Paul looked at his divine destiny that lay before him like a runner looks at the finish line. Rather than approach his spiritual race lazily and half-heartedly, Paul did everything within his power to preach the Gospel. If it meant getting a job on the side in order to be able to preach, that's what Paul did (Acts 18:3). If it meant becoming as a Jew in order to be able to preach to the Jews, that's what Paul did (1 Corinthians 9:20). And if it meant becoming as those without law to win those who were without law, that's what Paul did (1 Corinthians 9:21). He became all things to all men in order that he might win some to the Lord (1 Corinthians 9:22).

Paul suffered hardship, persecution, lack, cold, hunger, nakedness, homelessness, trouble from false brethren, trouble from true brethren — in the city, in the wilderness, and even at sea. He was beaten, afflicted by persecution, and troubled by religious people. Yet Paul never lost sight of the fact that he was called of God and that he would one day account for what he did with that calling. The finish line was always before him! He kept one thing foremost in his mind and preeminent in his thinking: *I must obtain the prize. I must fulfill the purpose for which I was born. I must achieve the plan of God for my life.*

Likewise, if you want to achieve God's will for your life, there isn't room for any other attitude than one of boldness and determination to keep running toward the goal with your eyes fixed on the finish line! This alone will take you through every obstacle and attack of the enemy and ultimately bring you to the place God desires for your life.

Like Paul, you must have resolve, strength of will, determination, backbone, high morale, courage, devotedness, persistence, tenacity, and an unrelenting mindset. You must put your foot down and take your stand as a no-nonsense kind of person who puts your whole heart into your calling. Sitting around hoping for something to happen isn't going to produce anything! You have to jump in the race, fix your eyes on the goal, and run with all your might to the finish line so you can take the prize!

It's time for you to "take the bull by the horns" and then hold on for dear life all the way to the goal! Make the decision that you are going to run the race, go the distance, and finish in first place! Only you can make this choice, so why not get started today?

My Prayer for Today

Lord, I ask You to help me become more fixed and focused on the goal You have given for my life. I don't want to allow distractions to pull me away from Your plan any longer. I want to shut my eyes and ears to the voices that beckon me to slow down and then set my face toward the purpose for which I was born. I can only do this with the help of Your Spirit, so today I turn to You to empower me to do this and to carry it all the way through to completion! I pray this in Jesus' name!

My Confession for Today

I confess that I am fixed and focused on God's plan for my life. I have set my face like flint; I am unflinching and unstoppable in my pursuit toward the goals God has set for me. I have strength of will, determination, a strong backbone, high morale, courage, devotedness, persistence, tenacity, and an unrelenting mindset. I have put my foot down and taken my stand. I am in the race; I have fixed my eyes on the goal, and I run with all my might so I can take the prize! I declare this by faith in Jesus' name!

Questions for You to Consider

1. How well are you running your race of faith right now? Are you consistent, or are you on-again, off-again in the way you are pursuing God's plan for your life?

____

____

____

____

____

____

2. If you keep running at the pace you're running right now, how long will it take you to get to where God wants you to be? Is it even possible to reach God's destination for you at your present pace?

____

____

____

____

____

____

3. What do you need to do to become more focused and less distracted? What do you need to remove from your life to help you stay on track and keep your sight fixed on the goal before you?

Day 26

Royal Ambassadors for Christ

> *Now then we are ambassadors for Christ....*
>
> — 2 Corinthians 5:20

Did you know that you have a high-ranking, esteemed, celebrated, impressive, and influential job in the Kingdom of God? It's true! You are so important to the Kingdom of God that all of Heaven is standing behind you, just waiting to back you up, defend you, provide for you, help and assist you, and join forces with your actions of faith! In short, Heaven is just waiting to act on your behalf. Why? Because you are an ambassador for Christ to this world!

In Second Corinthians 5:20, Paul wrote, "Now then we are ambassadors for Christ...." The word "ambassador" comes from the Greek word *presbeuo*. It describes "an ambassador" or "one who fulfills the duties of an ambassador." How wonderful that Paul would use this word to describe you and me!

In New Testament times and in today's world, the word "ambassador" has the same meaning. An "ambassador" can be defined as:

- An envoy sent to represent a nation to a foreign land.
- A diplomatic agent of the highest rank accredited to a foreign government or king.
- A representative temporarily sent to a foreign country to represent the king or country that sent him.
- An authorized messenger who has the power to make decisions and to represent the will of the government, nation, or king he represents.
- An official representative who is authorized to speak on behalf of their sender.

According to Paul's words in Second Corinthians 5:20, we are heavenly delegates — "ambassadors" who have been sent forth as Heaven's representatives to planet earth! As ambassadors for Christ, we are the voice of Heaven. As His representatives, we are authorized to speak and act on behalf of the Lord. And as Heaven's ambassadors, we are fully backed, fully funded, fully defended, and fully assisted by the authority and resources of Heaven!

Paul's words in Second Corinthians 5:20, therefore mean:

> *"We are sent forth and temporarily stationed here as the fully authorized representatives of Jesus Christ! As His ambassadors, we are here to be His voice and His will — a true representation of who He really is. As His official representatives sent here to do His business, we are fully backed up by all the power and resources of Heaven...."*

Don't ever think that you are unimportant to the plan of God. You are an ambassador! You represent Jesus Christ to your family, to your place of employment, and to your neighborhood. You have been invested with royal powers, including the name of Jesus and the authority of His blood, and you may call upon Heaven to assist you at any given moment! All angelic powers and all the vast resources stored in the treasury of Heaven are available for your use when you are representing Heaven to this world!

So wherever you go today and whatever you do, remember the One you are representing. If you need special help from above in order to represent the Lord in a positive way, remember that as an ambassador of Christ, all of Heaven is standing by to fully support you!

As your day gets started, stop for a moment and think about who you really are in Jesus Christ. You are a royal ambassador for the King of kings Himself!

My Prayer for Today

Lord, I thank You for the tremendous privilege of representing You on this earth! Please forgive me for the times I have overlooked the honor of being a child of God. I am sorry for the moments when I've been negative about myself, talked badly about myself, and did not acknowledge who You have made me to be in Jesus Christ. Today I am asking the Holy Spirit to help me see and truly perceive that You have made me to be an ambassador in this world! I pray this in Jesus' name!

My Confession for Today

I confess that I am important to the plan of God. I am an ambassador! I represent Jesus Christ to my family, to my place of employment, and to my neighborhood. I have been invested with royal powers, including the name of Jesus and the authority of the blood, and I may call upon Heaven to assist me at any given moment! All angelic powers and all the vast resources stored in the treasury of Heaven are available for my use when I am representing Jesus to this world! I declare this by faith in Jesus' name!

Questions for You to Consider

1. Have you ever viewed yourself as an ambassador of Jesus Christ?

2. Have you asked the Father to give you a revelation of your rightful place as an ambassador for Jesus Christ?

3. In what ways can you act as an ambassador for Jesus where you live and work?

Day 27

Early Beginnings

> *Moreover it is required in stewards, that a man be found faithful.*
>
> — 1 Corinthians 4:2

When the Holy Spirit first told us to begin our TV ministry in the former USSR, Denise and I had no idea what we were doing. We had never done a TV ministry before, and television equipment was not available to purchase in the Soviet Union. But with a small staff and a tiny budget — and a single home-video camera — we began to film the first programs of *Good News with Rick Renner.*

At that time, television programming on Soviet television was dark and bleak. Some of it was still broadcast in black and white. So even though we were filming with a home-video camera, the low-budget programs we produced looked at least as good as the other programs being broadcast on the Soviet stations.

Although we started in such a primitive fashion, I had great expectations for what God was going to do through this new television outreach.

Adding interest to the program was the fact that there were no Americans broadcasting on Soviet television at the time. When our faces appeared on TV sets across the huge region where we first broadcast, it was a breakthrough that had never occurred before. People were mesmerized that Americans were on their televisions, and people began to tune in to hear what we had to say. Most often, I was the only one on the program, but from time to time, Denise joined me as well.

At first, we began to notice that people recognized us when we went to the open market to purchase groceries for our house. They thanked us for our programs and reached out to touch us in a tender way, trying to express their thanksgiving for what we brought into their homes.

Then the letters started to pour in, taking us completely off guard. We had not anticipated such a huge mail response! The first book we printed and offered as a free gift on television was *Dream Thieves* — and when we made that offer, boxes upon boxes of mail poured into our offices. It was the beginning of a TV ministry that has continued for decades uninterrupted, right up to the present day.

My team and I had little knowledge of what we were doing. Our equipment was just an old, used home-video camera, and the lights we used to light up the "set" (our living room) were the lamps from our house. Yet God used the simplicity of it all and began the process of opening entire nations to the teaching of God's Word via television! It was a small beginning, but it was a beginning. Today this outreach has blossomed into a TV ministry that reaches not only the Russian-speaking nations of the former USSR, but people all over the world through satellite and the Internet.

When you start out with a new assignment from Heaven, you have to start with what you have and with what you know. Whether it is a business, a church, a ministry, or some other pursuit — you can only start at the level where you are and with the amount of money you have at your disposal. You must measure where you are, what stage you are in, and move cautiously and smartly as you proceed to obey and fulfill the call of God on your life. Denise and I weren't thrilled about starting our TV ministry with an old home-video camera and living-room lamps, but that is what we had and what we could afford. And because we were faithful with what we had, God blessed it and increased us over time.

In First Corinthians 4:2, Paul talked about faithfulness and people who are charged with overseeing projects, saying, "Moreover it is required in stewards, that a man be found faithful." As we were slowly building our TV ministry, my mind often went to this verse, because it clearly teaches that God watches to see if we are faithful with what has been entrusted to us. Being faithful wouldn't have been demonstrated by complaining that we had to use a home-video camera. Being faithful was making the decision that we'd cheerfully use that camera to its maximum potential! Faithfulness has a lot to do with attitude — it is not based only on performance.

Notice that Paul spoke of "stewards" in this verse. It comes from the Greek word *oikonomos*, which is a compound of the word *oikos* and *nomos*. The word *oikos* means "house," and *nomos* means "law." When compounded, the new word means "the rule or administration of a house." It could also be used to denote "the administrator of any project."

Such "stewards" had control of household finances and personal information about their employers; therefore, they had to be highly trusted individuals. Many "stewards" were highly educated and trained for years to attain such positions. However, most started as lowly servants and advanced to higher ranks over a period of time as they proved themselves faithful. Their superiors learned to trust them immensely because they had proven themselves faithful time and time and time again. Thus, a valued steward was generally thoroughly vetted and time-tested.

But First Corinthians 4:2 says, "...It is required in stewards that a man be found faithful." The word "found" is the word *eurisko*, and it depicts "a discovery that is made after a long period of study and investigation." The idea this word carries is that of a *successful conclusion* to a diligent search. After performing a long and arduous study of a person, carefully examining his behavior and ability to work and fulfill responsibilities, at last one determines that this person is "faithful."

The word "faithful" is the Greek word *pistos*, which in this particular case denotes "one who is utterly reliable." It is one who shows unchanging affection or support in the face of difficulty. It is allegiance to a superior or employer. It is unwavering support to a cause, person, or assignment. This is a person whom an employer can depend on — and a person God can count on to carry through an assignment to the end.

So if you are starting a project on a small level, as Denise and I did with the beginning of our TV ministry, I urge you to be faithful to the core. Be utterly reliable with what God has entrusted into your hands. What you demonstrate to God will determine whether He finds you prepared for advancement or deems it necessary to keep you at your current level.

Today, I see the vast impact our TV ministry is having, especially in the Russian-speaking nations of the world. But I have not forgotten that we started with a home-video camera and house lamps in our living room. Rather than complain, we used what God provided and made the most of it. God saw our efforts — and eureka! — By His grace, He found us faithful, advanced our TV ministry, and gave us better equipment to reach a larger audience. We give all the praise and glory to Him, because it was His grace that even enabled us to be faithful!

What is the task before you today? Are you starting small, as Denise and I did when we started our TV ministry in the former USSR? Never forget that Zechariah 4:10 admonishes us not to despise the day of small beginnings! So start where you are, use what you have, and be faithful to the task the Lord has given you. And as God watches you over a period of time and sees that you are utterly reliable to complete with excellence the tasks He gives, He will advance you; He will entrust more to you; and He will promote you! That is a biblical principle found throughout the Word of God — and you can be guaranteed that it's true for you!

My Prayer for Today

Father, help me to keep my eyes fixed on the task You have assigned to me. Help me to not complain that my beginning is so small, and teach me how to use this opportunity to learn everything I can before my venture grows larger. I know that You are with me — and You are watching to see what kind of steward I will be. So Holy Spirit, I draw upon Your mighty strength within me to rise up and help me be the best I can be. Most of all, I want to be found pleasing to the Lord and be one whom He can trust with much! I pray this in Jesus' name!

My Confession for Today

I confess that I am committed to being utterly reliable in every task that Heaven entrusts to my care. I will be faithful to use what I have to the best of my ability and to demonstrate to the Father that I do not despise the day of small beginnings. I take this beginning time as an opportunity to learn, to excel, and to prove to God that I am a man or woman He can trust! I declare this by faith in Jesus' name!

Questions for You to Consider

1. What is the task before you right now? You can only start out at the level where you are and with the cash that is available to you. Be faithful with what you have — stretch it as far as you can make it go, do excellently with what is entrusted into your hands, and believe that God will see it and give you an upgrade!

2. What Bible character had a small beginning but ultimately made a huge impact with his life? If you have time to do it, it would be good for you to make a list, because there are quite a few of them. This would be quite an encouraging assignment for your heart and soul!

3. Can you think of someone you personally know who started a dream on a small level, but worked and worked at it until it grew and became significant? Who is that person? What character traits does that person demonstrate that added to his or her success and that you would like to see added to your life?

Day 28

God Rewards Your Sacrifices

> *Therefore, my beloved brethren, be ye steadfast, unmoveable, always abounding in the work of the Lord, forasmuch as ye know that your labour is not in vain in the Lord.*
>
> — 1 Corinthians 15:58

I know that you face many demands, but today I want to remind you that God has watched what you have done for His work, and He will reward you. All the time, effort, and finances you have sown into the advancement of the Gospel are before His face — and He is faithful to remember and to reward you for what you have done. In First Corinthians 15:58, Paul wrote, "Therefore, my beloved brethren, be ye steadfast, unmovable, always abounding in the work of the Lord, forasmuch as ye know that your labor is not in vain in the Lord."

Notice especially the last part of the verse that declares your labor is not in vain in the Lord. The word "labor" is the Greek word *kopos*, which can refer to "the most exhausting kind of work or effort." Because this word is used in this context, it tells us that sometimes it is not easy to obey what the Lord tells us to do; sometimes it is very difficult to obey Him. In fact, there are times when it requires great effort to walk in obedience. But this verse promises that our labor has not been in vain!

I think of all the times the Lord has asked me to do something that was very difficult. Yet because I have always wanted to obey the Lord, I have done my best to follow His instructions, regardless of how hard it was or how much it required of my family or of me. Building our work in Russia has not been an easy task. But God called us to do it, so Denise and I and our sons have given 100 percent of our lives to this divine mandate. Since that is what God has asked of us, that is what we decided we were going to do.

Regardless of where you live or what you believe God has asked you to do, it is important that you give your whole heart and soul to your divine assignment. Even if it is difficult sometimes, you must keep pressing forward toward your God-given goal in obedience to the Lord. And whenever the way of obedience seems difficult, you need to remind yourself once again of His promise that "your labor is not in vain in the Lord."

The word "vain" is the Greek word *kenos*, and it depicts something that is "empty, void," or "wasted." This is God's promise that anything you do for Him is never a waste! When the devil tempts you to think that no one is noticing what you are doing or that no one appreciates what you do — that is the moment for you to remember that nothing done for the Lord is ever a waste! Every effort, every deed, everything you have ever done in obedience to Him will be credited to your heavenly record!

Don't let the devil discourage you. Dig in your heels and remind him that you are standing in faith on God's promises! Declare with confidence that God is going to be faithful to meet every need in your life because you have faithfully sown your time, effort, and finances. And never forget: Nothing you ever do for the Lord is a waste!

My Prayer for Today

Father, I am grateful for this reminder that You pay attention to my response to Your assignment for my life. You are very aware of where I am in life, and You see what I do to express faithfulness to You. Thank You for strengthening me with Your might in those times when I felt discouraged and wondered if my labor was in vain. I rejoice in Your all-sufficient grace that never fails to cover me in the midst of the difficulties and hardships I may encounter while obeying You. Lord, I ask You to help me be conformed more fully to Your faithful ways, so when my heavenly record is read before You, I will receive a crown to place at Your feet on that day. I pray this in Jesus' name!

My Confession for Today

I declare that I am steadfast, immovable, always abounding in the work of the Lord, because I know that my labor in the Lord is not wasted. God is aware of all that I say and do for His glory. He openly sees my heart's motivation for what I have said and done, and He will reward me accordingly. I do not live my life for the praises of man. The prize I seek is God's approval. Therefore, I set my focus daily to live a life that will matter for eternity as I labor to see the will of God done on earth as it is in heaven. I declare this by faith in Jesus' name!

Questions for You to Consider

1. Can you think of an area where you have labored especially hard for the Lord, and you've been tempted to think that it is all in vain? How did today's *Sparkling Gem* encourage you to keep going?

2. Would you describe your position of faith as being immovable, or have you been up and down in your walk of faith? What changes do you think you need to implement in your spiritual life to become more stable and enduring?

3. Do you have anyone who can stand in faith with you and encourage you as you wait for God's plan to come to pass in your life? Are they people who can pray with you and encourage you to dig your heels in deep until you see God's reward?

Day 29

Self-Discovery: Why God Tests You

By faith Abraham, when he was tried, offered up Isaac: and he that had received the promises offered up his own begotten son, of whom it was said, That in Issac shall thy seed be called: Accounting that God was able to raise him up from the dead....

— Hebrews 11:17-19

I know from firsthand experience that when God asks you to sacrifice something precious, it can be very difficult to come into compliance with what He is asking you to do. The flesh rebels every step of the way, and the mind tries to argue, as if it knows better than the Lord. Therefore, when your will collides with God's divine plan for your life, you must make a conscious decision to exercise obedience and follow His leading, no matter what.

There are critical moments when you must make the choice to do what God asks, whether or not you understand it. When you fully abandon your natural inclinations and defer to God's will, you will be elevated to brand-new levels of success and victory that you have never before attained.

Let me share an example of this kind of deference and obedience from my own life. When God first asked my family to move to the USSR, I knew He had something truly wonderful in store for us. However, my flesh didn't relish the idea one bit. Night after night, I lay in my bed and listened as my mind told me that this move was the stupidest notion I'd ever considered in my life and that if I really carried through with this absurd idea, I would lose everything. I was having an ongoing inner dialogue with God about the matter. I remember asking Him, Are You REALLY asking me to sacrifice everything that we've worked so hard to achieve?

At the time God called us to move overseas, our ministry in the United States was finally taking off after years of struggle and hard work. However, just as we were experiencing the first trappings of success, God asked us to lay aside our dream because He wanted to do something new through us. This was a pivotal moment in our lives! We didn't understand the full scope of His divine plan, so we had to choose to defer to His voice and trust that He was leading us on the right path.

Have you experienced a similar moment in your own life? If not, I guarantee you that a time will come when you will be called on to step out and follow God's leading, even though you don't fully understand His design. However, it is important to remember that when God asks you to sacrifice something precious in your life, He always has your best interest at heart, and He is trying to use that experience to reveal something to you about your life so that you can go forth and do the will of God with confidence.

A clear example of this biblical truth is clearly seen in the Old Testament story of Abraham. After waiting approximately 25 years for God's promise of a covenant child to come true, Abraham and Sarah finally became the proud parents of their son, Isaac. When Isaac was born, Abraham was 100 years old, and Sarah was 90 years old.

Everyone knew this baby was a miracle! How many 90-year-old women do you know who have given birth to a baby? It was so fantastic that even Sarah said, "God hath made me to laugh, so that all that hear will laugh with me. And she said, "Who would have said unto Abraham, that Sarah should have given children suck? For I have born him a son in his old age" (Genesis 21:7).

Try to imagine for a moment the sight of a 90-year-old woman breastfeeding a baby. You can understand why Sarah said everyone who saw it would laugh — it was absurd to the natural mind! Yet everyone who saw this mother and child together was filled with joy because it was such a demonstration of God's faithfulness to keep His Word. In fact, this blessing brought so many people joy that Abraham and Sarah named the baby Isaac, meaning laughter.

Abraham had personally given up a lot to accommodate the promise of God in his life. He knew that Isaac was the seed through whom God was going to bless the nations of the earth, as God had promised in Genesis 12:2-3 and Genesis 15:4-5. All of Abraham's hopes and dreams rested in Isaac.

However, after Abraham had spent years watching his son grow into a God-fearing young man, the Bible says that God came to him and commanded him to offer up Isaac as a burnt sacrifice! Genesis 22:1 and 2 records: "And it came to pass after these things, that God did tempt Abraham, and said unto him, Abraham: and he said, Behold, here I am. And he said, Take now thy son, thine only son Isaac, whom thou lovest, and get thee into the land of Moriah; and offer him there for a burnt offering upon one of the mountains which I will tell thee of."

In Hebrews 11:17, the writer of Hebrews offers another account of these events, saying, "By faith Abraham, when he was tried, offered up Isaac...." This verse tells us that God "tried" Abraham that day on Mount Moriah when He commanded him to sacrifice Isaac as a burnt offering on the altar.

This word "tried" is from the Greek word *peiradzo*, which describes "an intense examination that is done to prove the fitness of an object." For example, *peiradzo* was used to describe "the fiery process of testing and removing impurities from metal" in the ancient world. These tests ensured that the metal would be strong and durable, and that any object crafted from metal would hold up under pressure. In addition, *peiradzo* also described "the process of testing coins to determine if they were authentic or counterfeit." In early New Testament times, counterfeits often looked so similar to the genuine article that only a test would reveal whether a coin was real or fake. Therefore, people regularly tested their money to see if it had worth.

The word *peiradzo* most often described the process of testing an object to reveal its true quality, and this is precisely how the word is used in Hebrews 11:17, where the verse says Abraham was "tried" by the Lord. The fact is, the Lord already knew that Abraham's faith was sound and real. But when Abraham drew his knife to slay his son, Abraham himself learned something important about his own faith and level of consecration. He discovered that he was willing to do whatever the Lord asked him to do. There was nothing counterfeit or lacking about Abraham's obedience to God; his commitment was real and authentic.

You see, God never tests you to learn new information about you. He doesn't need to "test" to find out something new because He already knows it all. Rather, He is trying to show you something about you — to make you more self-assured and confident as you go forward to do His will. Every test you are going through is being done for your own self-discovery — lessons learned if you go through those tests correctly to give you confidence as you proceed to do the will of God for your life.

When God called my family to relocate to the former USSR back in 1991, my willingness to say yes to God revealed something to me about myself that I needed to see and know. It showed me that my commitment to God was real.

This experience was a *peiradzo* — a test designed to reveal the imperfect areas of my life that required attention and to prove to me that I was the type of person God could depend on. He already knew this about me, but I personally needed to know it deep down in my spirit.

I am so glad my family said, "Yes!" when God beckoned us to leave the United States and move to the former Soviet Union. Even though it initially felt like we were sacrificing everything to do it, the truth is, we didn't lose anything. What God has given us in our new home overseas is far greater than any home, possession, or dream that we thought we were relinquishing. From the very outset, God had a wonderful plan for the Renner family.

When God asks us to lay something on the altar of sacrifice, we can know there is something bigger and better He wants to put into our hands. But as long as we're clutching what we have right now, we're not free to receive the great things He wants to give us next.

Realize that whatever you're doing today may simply be the training ground for your future. Don't allow yourself to get so cemented in what you're doing that you can't move forward to the next step God has in store for you. And if it ever seems like God is asking you to make a huge sacrifice, just remember: This is just His way of freeing you so He can give you something better and greater and make you more productive for the Kingdom of God. You can trust Him! And as you keep your heart free and your emotions untangled, you'll be able to move forward whenever His Spirit beckons you to take the next step in His good plan for your life!

My Prayer for Today

Father, I am thankful to know that You already know everything about me and that You don't need to put me through a test to find out whether or not I'm genuine. Now I understand that You are trying to show me something about myself. Help me to embrace the tests that help me to learn what kind of person I am. Holy Spirit, I ask You to help me cooperate with Your working in my life so that I will become the type of person You can use to expand and build Your Kingdom. That is my heartfelt prayer. I pray this in Jesus' name!

My Confession for Today

I confess that I am alert to recognize when God is testing me to show me something I need to know about myself. He already knows all the answers about me, and nothing takes Him by surprise. But I need to know about me. I need to know that I am willing to obey and do whatever He asks me to do. I need to know that I am authentic and genuine in my faith. What He is asking me to do is for me to gain revelation about myself. It is information I need to know so that I can proceed with confidence and boldness as I push forward toward God's plan for my life. I declare this by faith in Jesus' name!

Questions for You to Consider

1. After reading today's *Sparkling Gem,* do you see that God tests you to reveal something to you about yourself? God already knows all the answers and doesn't need a test to find out something about you. So what do the tests you've undergone reveal about you that you need to know?

2. How do you think Abraham felt after he passed his test on Mount Moriah? What did he discover about himself and his own willingness to obey God?

3. What test are you going through right now? Do you now understand that God already knows the answers, and He's trying to show something to you about you? What is He trying to show you?

Day 30

Is it Time for a Personal Evaluation?

For unto every one that hath shall be given, and he shall have abundance: but from him that hath not shall be taken away even that which he hath.

— Matthew 25:29

A business consultant who gave high-dollar lectures to large companies once asked me, "Rick, how are you able to accomplish all that you do in your ministry? It seems like God keeps handing new assignments to you."

I was blessed by this man's view of our ministry, as he was a very serious businessman who had seen a lot over the course of his career. As I pondered his compliment, I was reminded of Jesus' teaching in Matthew 25:29, which says, "For unto every one that hath shall be given, and he shall have abundance: but from him that hath not shall be taken away even that which he hath." The word "abundance" in this verse is the Greek word *perisseuo*, which means "to abound" or "to have something in excess." In some places in the Greek New Testament, it carries the ideas of something that is given generously or something that is overflowing, plentiful, or even superabundant.

As I look back on all our years of ministry, I believe the word "abundance" perfectly describes the many assignments that God has given me. When it seems there is no more in us to take on new assignments, that is often when God opens a marvelous new door and beckons us to walk through it. These past adventures of faith and obedience have built a strong foundation for our ministry, which enables us to do more and more with the help of our well-trained team. Although there is still much room for growth, the strides we've made over the years in our personal lives, in our spiritual walks, and in the structure of our organization have put us on solid ground and demonstrated to the Lord that we are capable of doing more. So "more" is exactly what the Lord continues to give us!

In Matthew 25:29, Jesus teaches that how you perform in your current endeavor determines whether or not God gives you greater, more significant responsibilities in the future. God is watching you right now to see if you will prove yourself faithful in your present task because it shows Him whether or not you can be trusted with a big promotion. Your future is contingent on your attitude and job performance in the present!

Therefore, it's important that you take a thorough look at yourself and honestly evaluate your condition.

Ask yourself the following questions:

- Am I giving my present job 100 percent of my effort?
- If I were looking for someone to fill a position of great responsibility, would I want to hire someone who has my attitude and work ethic?

- Do I finish projects, or do I drop the ball along the way?
- Can I be trusted with money?
- Do I handle my money in a way that shows I appreciate its value and power?
- Does my life and attitude reflect the qualities that would make God want to choose me?

Your honest answers to these questions should help you determine whether or not you are the kind of person to whom God wants to give additional responsibilities in the future. Don't despair if your answers are less than satisfactory. Simply determine to make necessary adjustments in your life and become the kind of person God looks for when He needs someone to fulfill an assignment from Heaven!

One thing is certain: God does not choose lazy people who sit around doing nothing. Think about it. Why would He call someone to do His work when that person hasn't successfully done his or her own work?

There is not a single example in Scripture of God significantly using a person who was idly sitting around and wasting time when He called them. All the men and women of God in the Bible were already busy doing something when God spoke to them.

Consider Jesus' parable in Matthew 25:14-30, which tells of the master who gave talents to three of his servants. Jesus says that when the master returned from his long trip, he expected to see an increase and productivity as a result of his gifts. The two servants who were faithful and worked hard were richly rewarded. However, Jesus describes the servant who brought no increase or productivity as "unprofitable." The Greek word for "unprofitable" is *achreios*, which means "useless." It is the picture of a person who contributes so little that he is essentially worthless, and it reveals a lot about how Jesus views lazy people.

Through this parable, Jesus teaches that faithfulness and hard work are commendable in the Kingdom of God. When God needs someone to do something for Him, He looks for hardworking, faithful, "use-what-they-have" individuals who have already demonstrated worth. These people already know how to handle money; they know how to work; and they know how to stick with the job until it's done. Maybe they are still growing in these areas, but they have done enough to demonstrate to God that they can be trusted with more.

The Bible is loaded with examples of men and women of God who exude these qualities. The following list provides a few examples of strategic, well-known, key Bible personalities who were already successful before God called them, and there are many, many more found in Scripture.

- Noah was successful and righteous before he was called to build the ark.
- Abraham was successful and rich before God called him to become the father of faith.
- Joshua was successful as Moses' associate before God called him to be the leader of Israel.
- Gideon was successful as a leader before God called him to lead the Israelite armies.
- David was successful as a shepherd before God called him to be the king of Israel.
- Daniel was successful in Nebuchadnezzar's court and walked in integrity before God called him to be a prophet.

- Matthew was successful as a tax collector before Jesus called him to be His disciple.
- Peter was a successful fisherman and businessman before Jesus called him to be His disciple.
- Luke was a successful doctor before he was called into the ministry.
- Paul was a successful politician and religious leader before God called him into the apostolic ministry.
- Timothy was successful as Paul's associate and disciple before he became the pastor of the church of Ephesus.

This is just a small, representative list of the many similar cases I could show you from both the Old and New Testaments. God called these individuals because they had already proved their work ethic through their previous endeavors. By observation, He knew each of them could be trusted with a greater assignment.

You might try to put together a list of people who were doing nothing when God chose them for a big assignment. If you do, I believe you'll have a very difficult time assimilating such a list. I actually tried once to compile one, and I couldn't think of anyone who was used significantly by God but was doing nothing when He called him.

Maybe you think you have enough on your plate already, and that may be a fair point. But know that when God finds someone faithful, He likes to give that person more responsibility because He knows He's finally found someone He can trust. Therefore, don't be too surprised if more is given to you in "abundance." Just consider it the harvest of faithfulness and a demonstration of God's trust in you!

I encourage you today to conduct a deliberate self-evaluation to see how you're doing in your walk with God and where you need to grow and change. As God observes your willingness to yield to the necessary process of preparation, He will know when you are ready for more.

My Prayer for Today

Father, I pray that You will help me honestly evaluate myself and my performance. Even more, I ask for Your grace to help me see where I need to change. I receive Your empowerment to make the necessary adjustments so You can trust me with more responsibility. In those areas where I have not done well, I ask You to forgive me, and I receive Your forgiveness. With the power of the Holy Spirit and my decision to change, I believe that I'll make forward progress in my life and that You will put more on my plate because You've seen that I am faithful with what I'm doing right now. I pray this in Jesus' name!

My Confession for Today

I confess that I am faithful with what God assigned me to do right now. God is watching me; He is evaluating my performance, and He sees that I am doing the best I can with the knowledge and experience that I possess. I confess that I am willing to grow and change in the areas where I have not done well. I refuse to shut my eyes to the truth, and I will be honest with myself about the areas I need to change. God's Spirit is helping me — and with His help, I will become a vessel that God knows He can depend on and use. I declare this by faith in Jesus' name!

Questions for You to Consider

1. Take a moment to think about people whom God called upon to do great things. Can you think of any who were doing nothing at the time that God called them?

2. Based on the conclusion that God gives more to people who are doing well with what he has already given them to do, how do you evaluate yourself? Are you a candidate to whom God would consider giving more responsibility?

3. As you evaluate yourself honestly, what are the areas that you know need to change?

Day 31

Don't Get in a Hurry!

But as we were allowed of God to be put in trust with the gospel, even so we speak; not as pleasing men, but God, which trieth our hearts.

— 1 Thessalonians 2:4

Have you ever wondered, God, how long am I going to have to wait for that promotion I deserve? Is there a reason that the promotion I want keeps getting delayed? What is happening in my life, Lord?

We always seem concerned about making things happen faster, but God doesn't work in the same time frame we do. There are some things that are more important to God than giving us a promotion when we want it or making sure we get a pay raise when we think we deserve it.

Now, God does reward us for our faithfulness, but sometimes He takes a little longer than we might like to promote us in order to make sure we're really ready for that next big assignment. It's hard on the flesh while we wait, yet it is actually the mercy of God at work. You see, during that time of waiting, the imperfections that would have ruined us are exposed so God can remove them. Then He can move us up into the new position with no concern that a hidden flaw will cause us to fall flat on our faces.

We know from Acts 9:20-25 that when Paul first became a Christian, he tried to barge right into a public ministry. But he wasn't ready for that yet, and therefore created some problems and a lack of peace in the Early Church. Although saved and called, he simply wasn't ready to be promoted into such a visible position of leadership. It was going to take some time for God to prepare Paul for the kind of ministry and anointing he was going to carry in his life.

Paul referred to this process when he wrote to the Thessalonians. He said, "But as we were allowed of God to be put in trust with the gospel, even so we speak; not as pleasing men, but God, which trieth our hearts" (1 Thessalonians 2:4). This verse is packed full of insight regarding Paul's own experience of being prepared, tested, and finally promoted into his own public ministry.

Notice first that Paul says, "But as we were allowed of God...." The word "allowed" is the Greek word *dokimadzo*, a word that means "to test; to examine; to inspect; to scrutinize; to determine the quality or sincerity of a thing." Because the object scrutinized has passed the test, it can now be viewed as genuine and sincere.

This word, *dokimadzo,* was also used to illustrate the test used to determine real and counterfeit coinage. After a scrutinizing test was performed, the bona fide coinage would stand up to the test, and the counterfeit would fail. The strictness conveyed by the word *dokimadzo* is evident by an early use of this word to picture the refining of metal by fire to remove its impurities. First, the metal was placed in a fire that burned at a certain degree of heat; then it was placed in a fire burning at an even higher degree; and finally, it was placed in a blazing fire that burned at the highest degree of all. Three such tests were needed in order to remove from the metal all the unseen impurities that were hidden from the naked eye.

From the viewpoint of the naked eye, the metal probably looked strong and ready to be used even prior to those tests. But unseen defects were resident in the metal that would have shown up later as a break, a fracture, or some kind of malfunction. Before a person could be assured that the metal was free of defects and thus ready to be used, these three purifying tests at three different degrees of blazing hot fire were required. The fire was hot and the process was lengthy, but the tests were necessary in order to achieve the desired result.

Because Paul uses the word *dokimadzo*, he testifies to us:

> *"It was a lengthy process and I went through a lot of refining fires to get to this place, but finally I passed the test and God saw that I was genuinely ready...."*

So don't be discouraged if it takes time for your dream to become a reality in your life! God never gets in a hurry, because godly character is more important to Him than gifts, talents, or temporary success in the eyes of other people. He wants to use you, but He also wants you to be ready to be used!

Right now you may need some time to prepare, change, and grow. That way when God finally promotes you, you'll have what you need both naturally and spiritually to STAY established in that God-ordained position as you fulfill your assignment with excellence.

My Prayer for Today

Lord, thank You for considering my character so carefully. I know that You want to change me and conform me into the image of Jesus more than anything else. I often feel rushed to get things moving, but I know that You are looking to see if I have the character I need so I can successfully do what You've called me to do. I yield my heart to You and ask You to do Your work inside me. Change me so You can use me as You wish! I pray this in Jesus' name!

My Confession for Today

I declare by faith that I am being changed so God can use me to the degree He desires! Yes, I have areas in my life that need to be transformed, but because I renew my mind with the Word of God and spend time in prayer, God is free to work on me and get me ready for the big job He has designed for my life. I know that as I stay open and willing to change, my character WILL be transformed into the image of Jesus so I can complete my task successfully and to the glory of God! I declare this by faith in Jesus' name!

Questions for You to Consider

1. Do you think you're ready for a big new promotion?

2. If it seems like your promotion has gotten delayed again and again, do you have any idea why this might be happening?

3. Are there any areas of weakness in your life that could hinder you once you step into a more visible and demanding role? What are those areas you need to work on?

About Rick Renner

Rick Renner (renner.org) holds an earned ThD (Doctor of Theology) from a prominent Russian university and is a respected Bible teacher and leader in the international Christian community. He is the author of an extensive list of books, including bestsellers *Sparkling Gems from the Greek 1* and *2*, and his accumulated titles have sold millions of copies worldwide. Rick's understanding of the Greek language and biblical history opens up the Scriptures in a unique way that enables his audience to gain wisdom and insight while learning something brand new from the Word of God.

Today Rick is the overseer of the Good News Association of Churches, founder of the Moscow Good News Church, pastor of the Internet Good News Church, founder of Media Mir, and president of the Good News Channel — the largest Russian-speaking Christian satellite network in the world, which broadcasts the Gospel 24/7 to countless viewers in more than 83 nations. He is also founder of TBV, a national channel that broadcasts to all of Russia.

Rick is the founder of RENNER Ministries in Broken Arrow, Oklahoma, and host to his TV program, also seen around the world in multiple languages via television, Internet, and satellite. He leads this amazing work with Denise, his wife and lifelong ministry partner, along with their sons and committed leadership team.

Facebook: www.facebook.com/RickRenner

YouTube: www.youtube.com/RennerMinistries

Instagram: www.instagram.com/rickrrenner

Twitter: www.twitter.com/rennerrick

Harrison House Books by Rick Renner

A Life Ablaze

Christmas: The Rest of the Story

Dressed to Kill

Easter: The Rest of the Story

Fallen Angels, Giants, Monsters, and the World Before the Flood

How to Keep Your Head on Straight in a World Gone Crazy

How to Receive Answers from Heaven

Last Days Survival Guide

Life in the Combat Zone

Paid in Full

Renner A to Z

Renner Interpretive Version: 1 and 2 Peter

Renner Interpretive Version: James and Jude

Signs You'll See Just Before Jesus Comes

Sparkling Gems from the Greek 1

Sparkling Gems from the Greek 2

Spiritual Weapons to Defeat the Enemy

The Holy Spirit and You!

The Rapture, the Antichrist, and the Tribulation